ABOUT THE AUTHOR

I was born on the 13th of March, 1958. I am the son of Carlos and Amelia, brother of Patricia, Carlos and Jorge, husband of Maru, father of Mariana and Santiago, and uncle of Alan.

I have three novels published: *Guillotine Squad*, *A Sweet Scent of Death* and *The Night's Buffalo*. Also a book of short stories, *Retorno 201*, named after the street on which I grew up in Mexico City. In this street I picked fights all the time. When I was thirteen I had severe fractures to my nose and I lost my sense of smell.

Twenty years ago I had a car accident in the deep mountains of Central Mexico. I was sleeping in the back seat when it happened. Suddenly everything became chaos: metal breaking, windows shattering, shouts, blood, bones and then a frightening silence. Since then I have become obsessed with car accidents. So I decided to write about them in a trilogy of screenplays: *Upon Open Sky* – still not filmed – *Amores Perros* and finally *21 Grams*.

Car accidents, forbidden love, redemption, violence, revenge, characters walking the borderline of abyss, and the weight of dead people over the ones that survived them are my obsessions. I lost my grandmother, Guadalupe, when I was fifteen years old. I still remember her every day. I have tried to explain her absence to myself through all my work.

I have been a university professor for twenty-three years. I love teaching but I dislike academic life, I just cannot understand it. Teaching allows me to learn and to know what is inside the minds and hearts of other generations. I respect writers who like to tell stories and who use language to explore the human condition. I admire the work of William Faulkner, Shakespeare, Juan Rulfo, Martín Luis Guzmán, Pío Baro Montejo, Pedro Juan Gutiérrez, F Stendhal, García Márquez, Benjai Ellroy, Cormac McCarthy, Varga I detest writers who use words as write bland prose. I absolutely h contemporary need to be 'nice' al

GW00657832

Guillermo Arriaga, Mexico City, 2003

21 GRAMS

Guillermo Arriaga

Translated by Alan Page
Definitive English version by
Guillermo Arriaga and Alan Page

faber and faber

First published in 2003
by Faber and Faber Limited
3 Queen Square, London WC1N 3AU
Published in the United States by Faber and Faber Inc.
an affiliate of Farrar, Straus and Giroux LLC, New York

Typeset by Country Setting, Kingsdown, Kent CT14 8ES
Printed in England by Mackays of Chatham plc, Chatham, Kent

A CIP record for this book
is available from the British Library

ISBN 0–571–22266–8

2 4 6 8 10 9 7 5 3 1

FOR MARIANA AND SANTIAGO

with all my love

CONTENTS

Guillermo Arriaga

LIFE GOES ON

Guillermo Arriaga
interviewed by Kevin Conroy Scott

KEVIN CONROY SCOTT *You've worked with Alejandro González Iñárritu twice now. Can you tell me something about your first impressions?*

GUILLERMO ARRIAGA We first met through a common friend, Pelayo Gutierrez. I thought Alejandro was very human; he has an eye that can switch to several angles which helps to give him a deeper view of things. So when I say he is 'human', I am saying he is concerned with feelings and he is very compassionate. He is also very contradictory and that appeals to me.

What appeals to you about Alejandro being contradictory?

I think that the most interesting human beings are the ones who have a lot of contradictions because the more contradictions they have the more human they are. He has some points of view that are very different from mine, almost opposite. For example, I'm an atheist and he's very Catholic. I come from a very atheist family, my brothers and my sisters are atheists; my father is agnostic and comes from a very Catholic background. So those kinds of things are very interesting for me.

And what did you think of him when you first met? He was something of an impresario, a very successful DJ at a young age who went on to direct award-winning TV adverts. Then this young hotshot comes to you, a successful literary novelist, to help write his first feature film. It sounds like you two are from different worlds.

I had met him for two minutes and I asked him two very personal questions and he answered them in such a way that I thought, 'I want to work with this guy on something.' And more: 'I want this guy to be my friend forever.'

So it didn't bother you that he didn't have any experience making feature films?

He had a lot of success making commercials. Everything he touches he makes into a success. In Mexico he changed the way radio was made. He changed things in television advertising, too, and now he is changing the way films are made. He has an energy and a concentration to him that makes him different. I am absolutely convinced he is one of the great directors of our time and, of course, a great human being.

As initially written, 21 Grams *was set in Mexico City. Is that right?*

It was set in Mexico, not Mexico City. It was written in Mexican Spanish; I try to make my stories in such a way that they are very local but they can also be carried by any type of human being.

How did the project come together, then? Did you have a contract to make another film after Amores Perros?

No, we didn't have a contract. We only had a handshake.

So the idea was that you were going to make another film after Amores Perros?

We didn't know what was going to happen. Alejandro was being seduced by a lot of Hollywood producers who gave him lots of screenplays to consider directing. I wanted to give him a story so powerful that he would have no other option but to direct it. So I'm very happy with it; he's a guy I trust a lot. The idea for *21 Grams* is a very old idea. I was running late to my own birthday party and I was sure my wife was going to be very angry. So I thought, 'What if I tell her I ran over a family?' So I had that idea long before I finished *Amores Perros* – but it was just an idea. Then I published one of my books in Spain and I was on this train that goes from Seville to Madrid and I was sleeping and then suddenly the idea came. The ideas for my films and my books always come from my dreams; I think the subconscious is much more intelligent than the conscious. So I came up with a clue to writing this film and it was a heart. So I thought, 'What happens if someone runs over a man and his small daughters and that man gives his heart to another guy?' Then *21 Grams* came to me.

Twenty-one grams is the amount of weight a human loses when they die. That's interesting, especially with you being an atheist; do you think this film is meant to have any kind of spiritual undertones to it?

The film is written by an atheist, but directed by a Catholic so I am sure Alejandro will try to give the film a spiritual resonance. I tried to give it an earthy feel, a very human thing, because for me life ends when you die. This twenty-one grams of weight that we lose, this can be energy, it can be the soul, it depends on your beliefs, it can be a lot of things. I used it as a metaphor for how this weight still weighs on the one who survives because sometimes someone is much more important dead than alive. Sometimes the living ones cannot overcome the death of someone they love. It has been thirty years since my grandmother's death and I still have not overcome it, it still hurts me. Those twenty-one grams of her are still weighing on me.

Getting back to the screenplay . . . it was written in Spanish and set in Mexico, then it was given to Alejandro. Was it his decision to make it in America?

It was a shared decision between the two of us.

How did the screenplay change after this decision was made?

It didn't change very much. What makes me very happy is that one of the actors, Melissa Leo, told me that I wrote an American film. Of course, I tried to have a more Americanised version; my translator, Alan Page, helped me a lot with that. That was not only in the dialogue but also in setting it in the right places. But the essence of the screenplay remained even after being translated.

What about understanding Christianity and reborn Christians? Those are very American elements.

The idea of the reborn Christian comes from a summer I spent with my wife and my kids in Brownsville, Texas. The character of Jack came to my mind before I was writing there. It was a completely different character and it wasn't working; at the time he was a businessman. So I was driving along with my wife and my children, crossing the Mexican Central Desert, and it was raining and everyone was sleeping in the car, and then it came to me, 'I have it, I have it! He'll be a car thief and a reborn Christian.' Then we arrived in Brownsville and it is full of reborn Christians. I hate doing research; that's why I prefer to write my own original screenplays. So instead of going everywhere to research this character

I just tried to imagine what his position would be. Also, I studied acting for a long time, so I thought about how this would affect me if I was an actor.

So you thought about the character of Jack from an actor's point of view?

No, from a writer's point of view: 'What would I do in the place of that man?' One of my best friends in Mexico became a reborn Christian and he stopped being my friend. He was an atheist and suddenly he got married to a reborn Christian and she said, 'Anyone who is not with us is part of the devil. You must not talk to anyone else, only the people who are from the born-again Christian community.'

Why do you think reborn Christians are so vocal about their beliefs? It is almost as if they are trying to sell their religion to people who are not of the same faith.

I think faith is very difficult to understand and the only way to make things understandable is words. When you experience a great passion, you need words to explain it. That's why I think they need to explain to everyone what their religion is about.

Do you think it relates to cinema audiences and their need to have aspects of a narrative explained to them, to be reassured by storytelling the same way that religion reassures people?

No, because the narratives expressed in films and books go through the more basic experiences of human life. Narrative can be understood through actions or images. That doesn't happen with religion. In order to understand it, you have to explain it through words. You cannot get the power of faith only through actions. You must explain it to the ones who don't live your same faith.

With a character like Paul, who has a voice-over – which to me suggests that he has some kind of religious or spiritual awareness – do you think he is concerned about what will happen to him when he dies?

In my particular point of view, I think he is more concerned about those who will survive. I think he has sacrificed himself to save the woman he loves.

If he is interested in the legacy that survival guarantees with Cristina, then why he is so against letting Mary have his child?

In the beginning he's against it because he's dying and he has a very bad relationship with her. I think you want to be a father with a woman you trust and you really love and you think there's some hope there. But he thinks it's over with Mary and that he's dying. But it's different with Cristina because she is a woman in pain and the only way to save her is by giving her motivation and hope. A baby gives hope, even though he doesn't know that he has made her pregnant. Many people who have read the script have asked why he shoots himself. It's very easy to understand. He's going to die because of his failed heart transplant, so if he shoots himself it will be so powerful that it will stop any further violence. If he shoots the gun into the air maybe they'll stop for a moment, I don't know. But if he shoots himself he knows that his action is so sacrificial that there will be no further violence between Cristina and Jack.

I read something on a website about 21 Grams *that related to this moment in the film. Someone had seen an early cut of the film and had given a positive review but with one objection: 'Paul's voice-over at the end of the film attempts to paint an almost positive viewpoint, urging the viewer to think about life and the fact that even though you and those you love can die at any time, you should cherish life and make the most of what you have. And yet the character we're focusing on for the end of the film has just committed suicide. That strikes me as contradictory. We could have focused on Jack or Cristina, both of whom are at positive turning points in their life because of Paul's sacrifice, but instead we focus on the character who killed himself. Why?'*

First of all, I am happy that this person used the word 'contradictory'. For me contradiction is the epitome of human nature. Many people in films want to make everything clear. I have been working with people and they say, 'Why this, why that?' and I answer, 'Because we are contradictory, paradoxical beings.' Many human acts cannot be understood if they are not under the light of contradiction, not under logic. Of course Paul sacrifices himself, but he is dying. He is going to die in the next minute or sometime in the near future. It's made clear that his heart is no longer working and that he's having a heart attack at that moment and the only method he has of taking the attention of Cristina away from killing Jack is for him to shoot himself. I think of it as an act of love.

Why do you use a voice-over for Paul when Jack and Cristina have no voice-over?

When the idea came to me, this was not the structure I had in mind. I have an old and unfinished novel that I wrote when I was twenty-five or twenty-six that has a structure that begins with a guy dying who says, 'So this is death's waiting room. All of these tubes, all of these needles, what am I doing here in this pre-corpse club?' That's how the novel begins and I thought I would use it. It's basically Paul's point of view, he's the one who makes the ultimate sacrifice, that's why I think he can have the voice-over. It's difficult to explain why, really, it was a poetic decision to have him explaining his feelings. You know when we speak in real life we don't go from A to B to C to D. For example, if I want to tell you about how I met my wife I would begin with yesterday, then go back to three years ago and then to when my first child was born. You go back and forth in time and I wanted to have this point of view of someone dying, going back and forth in time.

The fragments of the story, showing glimpses of the future, moments of the past, while not really showing what the present involves, seem devilishly difficult to construct. How did you go about solving the problems of chronology?

I think a good narrator can tell a story any way he wants if, in the end, he knows what's going on and it moves him and creates some big emotion inside himself. I have no problems structuring time in my mind because I think a little bit like that. What I was trying to make was a yin–yang, balancing things. Maybe people won't get it, but in the screenplay the first thirty-five pages have light, the scenes are mostly during day; then it becomes night for the next thirty-five pages, then it becomes day. I think that light creates emotional states and I tried to achieve these states throughout the screenplay. I was also balancing exterior and interior scenes, very carefully putting one scene with the other. I think that when you have one scene by itself it has one meaning. When you have one scene preceded by another and it is itself preceded by another scene, it changes the context of the scene completely. So I was very careful to have these symbolic and poetic linkings.

Can you give me a specific example of this in the screenplay?

One scene that I like very much is when Cristina is swimming with her sister Claudia and the cellphone rings and Cristina answers it. Cristina leaves the pool and says goodbye, and when she is walking out her sister calls her, 'Cristina!' We don't know what this is but at the end of the film, when this scene is put with the other ones, we then know that when Claudia shouts 'Cristina!' it's the exact moment that Cristina's family is dying. So when you have those scenes at the end of the film and you have the kids going out of the soda shop and you are seeing Jack saying goodbye . . . look at my arm.

Goosebumps.

Goosebumps. Because I was remembering that scene, that's the moment you suddenly realise what has happened to her family.

Getting back to how the film was made . . . I think it is safe to say that you and Alejandro think of yourselves as Mexican filmmakers before Hollywood filmmakers. Have you received any flak for not making your follow-up to Amores Perros *in Mexico?*

Some people criticised us for working in the United States. I don't understand it because I think that I'll be Mexican in every film I make whether it's in Chinese, Belgian, American or French. I think that's why they hire me in the States, because they want another point of view. They want another angle on things. Even though I can make very American films, I think they know I will see American society from another point of view.

Is there some way you can distil that Mexican-ness and try to give me a description of what that is?

We have contradictions here in Mexico, they're everywhere. This is a very powerful country in terms of culture. The culture in this country is amazing and very interesting. There's a contradiction between the history of the Indian and the Spanish, between the poor and the wealthy, the jungle and the desert. There are a lot of contradictions in Mexico and, as a result, it makes you feel that human beings are more contradictory.

The city of Memphis is not named in the screenplay but it's where the film was shot. The screenplay gives very little by way of scene description; it just gives us the barest descriptions of where we are. It's almost as if you are saying it's not important where we are, only that it's important to understand the structure we are in. Would you agree with that?

For me the background is very important. In my writing I specified that there were white chairs in front of Jack's house. When we were looking for locations, we suddenly saw a house with a white plastic chair in front of it. Also, I wrote about orange chairs being in the clinic and they were there too, you know. It's because sometimes when we tend to talk about background we want to speak about global backgrounds. I think that you can speak in a much more interesting way about background using little details, like the chairs. I am happy that the locations we found had the type of chairs I described in the screenplay, it's important.

How involved were you in the location process? I know you have been involved in the editing process.

Alejandro and I have a constant dialogue that goes through the whole process. I was invited to the location scouting and to see the editing process because Alejandro considered my thoughts as the writer and as his friend. He considers my point of view and he is very respectful. But the final decisions on the film were taken by him. It is he who is clearly the director and I am clearly the writer. Of course, Alejandro participated in the process of the screenplay. But it is I who take the final decisions concerning the screenplay. So this is a collaboration based on the respect we have for each other's work.

I read an article quoting Alejandro, which said that you and he had some difficulty developing the screenplay and that at one point you and he were at odds about in which direction to take it. What were you disagreeing about?

I really don't remember it that way. It is very difficult to be a very successful director who is making his second film. I don't think he was sure that it was the best one for him. So I was telling him all the time, 'It's really good, trust me, it's a good one.'

I would imagine that if he is being approached by successful producers with quality material then he might have trouble pulling the trigger on a target, especially being aware of the sophomore jinx that affects many successful first-time directors.

I know of many first-time directors who haven't even been able to make a second film. And now Alejandro has directed what I consider a great second film and I am very proud of him.

The structure of Amores Perros *is similar to* 21 Grams, *not only in the obvious way of having a car crash being the central intersection of the plot, but also in the way that the narrative runs backwards and forwards in time. Were films like* Rashomon *an influence?*

I think that *Amores Perros* and *21 Grams* have very different structures and themes; they are part of a Mexican trilogy I wrote involving car crashes; they are the second and third films, respectively. The first film I wrote begins with a car crash, but that hasn't been made yet. It is called *Upon Open Sky*. My major influences come from life and then from literature. In my screenwriting William Faulkner and William Shakespeare are my major influences. I learned from Faulkner that every story has a way to be told and that you have to take risks. From Shakespeare I learned that characters work better when they have stronger motivations and live in tough circumstances. And also that you have to take risks. By the way, Guillermo in English is William.

Let's talk about Cristina, played by Naomi Watts. She is a mother of two in some scenes and a drug addict in others. Why was she was a drug addict and why was that important?

I wanted to have the three characters come from three different hells. Cristina comes from the hell of drug addiction, Jack comes from the hell of prison and Paul comes from the hell of bad health and a dying heart. Each person has a moment where they think they are out of that hell and have reached the sky. Then they go back to that hell and have to overcome it again because hope is one thing in an easy-going life but having hope when you are in the depths of darkest place, that is a real sense of hope. I wanted her to be a drug addict because she was going through a lot of things. I think people of her age, in many parts of the world, are on drugs of one kind or another. I have a lot of friends that have died or are having problems because of drug addiction. Overcoming that because of love is very difficult, then to lose everything you have and to go back to the hell of drug addiction and then come back again and have hope through love is even more difficult.

Why do you think Cristina let Jack off the hook on his pending conviction for killing her family? He even confessed to driving the car that killed her husband and daughters.

I think when you're dealing with deep pain everything loses its sense, even revenge. This kind of pain brings you into numbness; it's so great you cannot even name it. There is no word for a person who has lost their child. A child who has lost their parents is an orphan, a woman who has lost her husband is a widow – but what do you call a parent who has lost their child? The pain is so big you cannot name it. I think that it's not that she lets Jack walk away. I think the pain is so big that Jack's guilt or innocence cannot even register with her. Her pain is so big that even revenge gets numbed. As I say with my novels, my characters lose their north and their south, their left and their right. This is what happens to Cristina.

She has lost her compass.

Exactly.

Why do you think Jack turned to Christianity in prison? He is so absolutely sure of his faith that it almost ruins his marriage.

The background of Jack is a guy who has been in jail for a long time. Prisoners sometimes have a lack of love when they are young, a lack of a sense of community and a lack of identity. If there is something that can give an inmate a sense of community with someone, an identity, and to be loved by someone, then they are going to be open to it. I think that the weaker you are, the more potential you have to fall into one of these sects. It happens a lot with prison inmates, they turn to Jesus. They are weak; they have no hope in life. Some people think that jail is something funny; that experiencing it is part of life. But filming in jails in Memphis was . . . there was no hope, there are people there who are very mean. So if suddenly someone comes to you and tells you that there is hope and there is love, of course you will want to be a part of that. That's how I feel about Jack. He's someone who needs to be pampered and loved. But his hope is very primitive. He has no structure in his mind to really understand it. He is very mechanical.

Bencio Del Toro plays the role of Jack in the film. Did you talk to him at all about playing the character? It's a very challenging role.

Of all the actors, he was the one I had the most relationship with. I think he is a great actor; he made a wonderful job of it. And I must say that I am absolutely touched by the great work of all the cast. Sean, Naomi, Melissa, Charlotte, Eddy were just amazing.

It's a very complicated role; he goes through a wide range of emotions. For example, he carves a tattoo out of his forearm with a knife, but then he also comes home from prison and tries to tenderly make love to his wife again, but without success.

It's contradictory. If someone wants to use a word for my characters it's that they are contradictory.

Paul is played by Sean Penn . . . the way he puts his heart in a glass jar and keeps it, it's almost as if his feelings and actions are tied up with his most prominent organ. As soon as someone else's heart is put in him, it's almost as if that person's feelings are transferred to him. Is that something you would agree with? Paul is with Mary, gets a transplant and falls for the donor's wife.

The other day I had a conversation with a cardiologist. He said it is strange, but it seems that cells retain some kind of memory. Sometimes people who have heart transplants will go into the house of the donor and they will know exactly where things are.

You can't be serious.

He told me that. I have no way to demonstrate it scientifically, but that's what he told me. Some scientists think that cells have memory.

Were you worried at all that Paul's interest in Cristina would be too much? In some ways he has fallen for her but in other ways he is stalking her.

I'm never concerned about likeability with my characters. Never, never. I am only concerned with making interesting characters. I think that audiences are much more sophisticated and diversified than we give them credit for. I think there is a kind of filmmaking that can relate to a very intelligent audience. Here in Mexico, when I wrote *Amores Perros* some people said to us that it would be difficult to make because no one would be interested in financing it. This was because it was not politically correct because of the dog-fighting, but it ended up being a blockbuster. There are no likeable characters in *Amores Perros*; each one of them is a son of a bitch.

Each one of them does something pretty awful, but each one of them has some redeeming qualities as well.

That's the contradiction. I am much more concerned with the contradiction of the characters; it makes them more human and interesting. I think the more contradictory they are, the more human they will be; the more human they are the more appealing they will be. What is very important in my writing is hunting. All of my characters hunt. Paul is hunting, he is a stalker, he hunts. As in *Amores Perros*, El Chivo, he hunts. He is stalking all the time.

At the end of the film Cristina is pregnant, Mary is pregnant and it is assumed that Paul is dead. Life goes on. In fact, 'life goes on' is something you used twice in the script in the characters' dialogue. I was wondering if that was a deliberate attempt at putting forth a theme.

It wasn't deliberate. I suddenly realised it was there after I wrote it and, as a result, so was the theme of the film. Life goes on, life goes on.

Is Paul's metamorphosis through open-heart surgery a personal issue with you? You had a life-threatening heart virus when you were in your twenties that made you want to become a writer.

The kind of illness I have in my heart, the disease is not supposed to be very serious. When I was boxing in my twenties and exercising a lot, it got swollen and my cardiac muscle was affected. I spent several weeks in bed. In that moment I realised that I wanted to make something that would transcend me and that's the exact moment I decided to be a professional writer.

Of course, this experience has a lot to do with the character of Paul. I tried to give Paul's character the feeling of pain, fear, hope, courage, anger, that I experienced myself.

So there is a link there?

Of course, it drives *21 Grams* all the way. I thought to myself during the time of my illness, 'What if I have to have someone else's heart?' It's terrifying. They stop your life and take your heart out. There is a moment in your life when you are empty. You have no heart and then you have the heart of a different person. I was also very affected by a photograph in *Life* magazine where I saw a guy staring at his heart in a jar. You are suddenly seeing your own heart. The heart that pounded for you when you were scared or happy is now in a jar. And now you are taking the heart of some-one who had a different life, with different emotions. And of course the heart is the most romantic of the organs. It's not the same as having a kidney or a pancreas transplant. [*Laughs.*]

You couldn't really pull off this movie with Paul getting someone else's pancreas, could you?

No. [*Laughs.*]

So Paul's heart is really the emotional heart of the film.

Exactly.

It's one thing to talk about likeability with a character, but it's another thing to talk about believability in the story. Were you ever worried that an audience might find it hard to believe that Cristina would make love to the man who had her dead husband's heart?

I think that it would be the most possible thing for a woman to do this. First of all Paul is a nice guy, he's attractive, he's intellectual, he's funny, he's tender and he's nice *and* he has the heart of her husband. Now she can now have a relationship with this guy who is all of those things and also the man who has a part of her hus-band. She has two in one.

21 Grams has a car accident, a heart transplant and some other pretty tough stuff. Then Paul comes along and falls for Cristina and gives her a funny speech about how he can be trusted. In a way, it is almost like a scene from a romantic comedy amidst this intense drama. How did you feel about having Paul make a speech like that so late in the film? Was it hard to change the tone so late in the script?

I don't think it's a change of tone. Paul is not going through what Cristina is going through. In the end Paul is grateful to Jack because, if it weren't for him, he would not be alive. So he's going through this aspect of life where he now has hope, so his character is in another place from Cristina, tonally. He is recovering from open-heart surgery, which is very intense, but it is not as intense as what Cristina has just been through. So Paul wants to do something for her. Not only that: when he follows her to the convenience store, he realises that he likes her a lot and he is grateful to her because she authorised the heart donation; without her he would be dead. He knows he has to relate to Cristina, but he doesn't knows how to approach her. He tries to be charming, to get her attention, even with that clumsy speech and his bad jokes. So it is not too much to think that his charm could win her over.

Do you think Paul is motivated by guilt?

No, he is motivated by gratefulness and then love. He wants to show his gratitude to the family that saved his life and then he falls in love with Cristina.

I came across a website that was predicting who will be nominated for the Academy Award next year for Best Original Screenplay in 2004. Your name was mentioned for 21 Grams. *How are you finding all this, the transition from Mexico to Hollywood?*

I have been preparing for this all of my life, since I was a kid. I always wanted to be a writer and tried my best. But when things really happen, you feel like you have been knocked by a giant wave and when you are swimming out to grasp some air, another giant wave strikes you. So my preparation consists in swimming as hard as I can and not getting drowned.

Has the success and interest in your work surprised you?

Of course it has surprised me. It is one thing to deserve something and it is another thing to achieve it. [*Laughs.*] It's like when you are playing basketball and you throw the ball from mid-court. Your intention is to score, and when you make it, you jump up and down because you're happy.

But making a mid-court shot doesn't happen that often, does it?

This is true. That's why it surprised me.

How would you describe the tone of your work?

I want my stuff to reflect the streets and the fields. When you read something of mine I want you to say, 'This guy was on that street and he was in that field. He was in the mountains, he was in the desert. He was there.'

He was on the battleground where life was won and lost. You were hunting out in the fields or you were boxing on the streets.

Exactly. I have my scars – and scars are important to tell stories.

Hollywood must appreciate you because your characters don't mess around, they get to the point very quickly and, like Hemingway and Faulkner, you don't mess about with adjectives, just action.

[*Laughs.*] What is very good for me with all this new work is my family. I remember when *Amores Perros* was nominated for Best Foreign Film. I was jumping up and down, I was very happy, of course. And my daughter says to me, 'Come on, Dad, don't make such a big fuss. You're just a nominee. When you win you can make a big fuss, right now you are just a nominee.' [*Laughs.*] My wife and my kids are everything to me.

Do you really think 21 Grams *is a film of hope?*

21 Grams is a metaphor for life. I think we always want to get hope through what are called 'feel-good' movies. But I think that you can get the importance of hope and love and life from intense and dark things. You can go through life and go through some tough phases and get hope from that. So yes, I think *21 Grams* is a film of hope.

And life goes on . . .

The power of life is much, much bigger than the power of death. That's not my quote; that's a quote from García Márquez.

Mexico City, Mexico, July 2003

Guillermo Arriaga and Alejandro González Iñárritu

DON'T BE AFRAID OF DEATH

Alejandro González Iñárritu
interviewed by Kevin Conroy Scott

KEVIN CONROY SCOTT *Why did you want to work with Guillermo Arriaga on your first feature film,* Amores Perros?

ALEJANDRO GONZÁLEZ IÑÁRRITU I read Guillermo's screenplay called *Upon Open Sky* – which is still unproduced. At the time I was developing a project by myself – writing a story – so I was looking for a screenwriter to work with. A friend of mine sent me *Upon Open Sky* and I immediately felt that this guy had an idea of how to write. It wasn't pretentious, it wasn't boring and it was also very deep at the same time. Sometimes when people pretend to write about deep matters they tend to get very preachy or very pretentious or very boring. This guy was talking about something very deep, but in an entertaining way. So we had lunch and we got on very well and ended up becoming friends.

What were your first impressions of Guillermo?

It's funny because when you see him he can look like a very bad man, like a tough guy who you wouldn't want to mess with. But then, when he speaks, you realise that he is a sweet man. What I know for sure is that he has a big heart and is a supernatural talent. I love that he has that façade to him. I also love the fact that he has been a teacher for so long and that he loves being at the university. By the way, our first argument was about that. I didn't believe in cinema studies at university because I thought all my teachers were very bad, except for a few. I think that most of the time they kill the students' intuition and innocence. Coincidentally, when I was studying cinema at the university in Mexico City, Guillermo was lecturing there at the same time. I was unhappy, so I called for a meeting with the faculty to complain about how bad the level of teaching was. Immediately Guillermo said, 'You were the one who called for that conference, who wrote that article in the newspaper!' And I said, 'Yes, I am.' He was angry and said things like, 'I have been teaching for twenty years!', but in the end he gave in and said, 'I understand what you were talking about.'

After the success of Amores Perros, *you were given a lot of offers by successful Hollywood producers who wanted you to direct their screenplays. Why did you decide to go with Guillermo's screenplay for* 21 Grams, *instead of all those other projects?*

The first reason was because I had a great experience working with him on *Amores Perros*. I trusted him and we developed a sense of working together during that time. As a director I feel that I want to be involved with a project from the first line that is written because I'm going to be giving three years of my life to it. If you build a house, you want to know the piece of land and see how the machines are going to be digging up the ground; you want to work with the architects from the beginning. You want to plan how each room is designed or how the bathroom is going to look or where your chairs are going to go. So being part of that process is what makes me feel excited. I also learn more about the film than at any other time because I begin to live with the characters; I begin to have positive and productive arguments with him. I don't think Guillermo is afraid of the human condition or to expose it without being ashamed of it. He's also an amazing writer of dialogue. He's very subtle, dry and contained. I decided to work with Guillermo because of the first experience I had with him and because of all of his values and talent. More importantly, I didn't find any other material that was more interesting than what I was doing with Guillermo at that time. There's nothing like working with talented friends.

He told me that usually he goes through ten drafts of a screenplay before he actually considers it to be his first draft and that he made a mistake in showing you his actual first draft and that he wished he wouldn't have done that. Do you remember your reaction to that first draft?

Yeah, it wasn't a good start, but nevertheless, that 'mistake' showed us the way that we shouldn't direct the story of the film. So now, looking back, maybe that was the best thing that could've happened. From that point forward, I was more aware of everything.

I read in some advance press for the film that you and Guillermo had some difficulty developing the screenplay. Do you remember what the major creative differences were during that time?

In terms of developing the screenplay, I think the process that Guillermo and I went through was very complex. At times, we found that our opinions differed in terms of how we envisioned the development and roots of a specific character or the structure itself. But we are used to getting through difficult processes. I don't think that any good script has been written and developed easily. If you want to climb to the top of a mountain, you have to sweat. I believe in 'no pain, no gain'.

So being friends with Guillermo and respecting his writing helped in constructing a ground-breaking narrative?

That's what I feel is best about working with Guillermo. He really allows me to work with him and to argue with him. That is a very productive thing for the script and the film.

So the creative arguments were a good thing?

When Guillermo and I were discussing this, I think we both learned more about the project. I lived with my characters for a long time before I began shooting, so when I was directing and an actor was going through an emotional exploration, I had already been there several times, rationally as well as emotionally. Also, as Guillermo made observations during the pre-production and even in the production of the film, his questions, points of view and suggestions really helped me to make my work better and to be more rigorous with myself.

So your writing experience is much more personal?

I cannot imagine how you can shoot a film like this if it's not personal. The physical and emotional costs are too high to make this kind of film as a director for hire. Films should be motivated by that which is intrinsic and personal.

Guillermo told me that he's an atheist and you're a Catholic. Can you tell me something about how this contradiction manifested itself in the development process?

We always have a personal joke, which is: I tell him that he is the most Catholic atheist that I have known in my life. He's a true believer, he just doesn't know it. He then tells me that I am the most devilish Catholic that he has ever met.

I have a lot of contradictions, but I truly believe in God. I see life as a spiritual journey. I feel that if life was just a physical journey, it would be very poor because we would be limited by our senses, by what our eyes and ears tell us. Reality is beyond our limited mind. I only know what is happening in this fucking room, but if this was all my world it would be fucking horrible, so I have to have faith. I have to have faith that my kids and my wife are breathing now, that they are alive, even though I can't see them in front of me. They are in Mexico now, but I have to have hope that they exist, that they are smiling. My senses don't allow me to see this, so hope and faith guide a lot of our life, every day, consciously or unconsciously, rationally or irrationally, religiously or pragmatically. The film is about loss and how, in order to survive, these characters find hope again through a painful process. Being that life can be so difficult and painful at times, I think that hope is the only way, as a human being, to give meaning to our life. So in terms of the script, I always felt that the journey of Jack should be more spiritual, rather than just legal or criminal. I always wanted this character to carry guilt along with him.

And guilt is a very Catholic emotion; anyone who has seen a Martin Scorsese film can tell you that.

Yes, I was born into a guilty culture, so I understand that very well. It can be a very destructive feeling, but at some point guilt can trigger some interesting actions. I am a true believer in interior journeys and I thought that the problem with Jack was that he was involved in a small fundamentalist congregation, which is very common nowadays. Look at how many 'sub-religions' have developed. People like to have an emotional need and sometimes they fill this need with very fundamentalist beliefs about something, whatever it is. It's a 'fast-track' solution, normally very close to the senses . . . smells, music, colours. As a result, their spirituality becomes very emotional. Their spirituality becomes subordinate to their emotions so if they don't cry in church, or if they don't feel the presence of something, they won't believe, because if they don't feel they won't believe. I think spirituality is beyond our senses and has to be more about serenity and peacefulness. Unfortunately, some people use religion to justify bombing other countries and others to practise terrorism.

Wasn't it also about Jack finding his religion while in prison? In prison you are so lonely that belonging to a group where love is promised seems like a good alternative to the horrible loneliness of prison life?

Completely. Marx said that a long time ago. Sometimes religion can be addictive, the same way that people can be addicted to a therapist or a psychiatrist or to drugs, alcohol or cigarettes. This is a film that has a lot to do with addictions. Cristina is an ex-addict and after the accident she goes back to the hell of that addiction. Jack was in hell, confronting his demons, and he got addicted to that emotional spirituality, trying to balance his life. But when the crash happened, he returned to hell and had to confront his demons once again.

How did 21 Grams *come together as a project? I believe there was a bidding war at one point, or at least several studios were making offers at the same time. That must have been unprecedented, for a Mexican writer–director partnership, making their first film in Hollywood, to have this kind of situation.*

I think that I just spent the right amount of time to get the script and the project in the best possible condition and that it gave me time to be prepared to begin the journey and, to tell you the truth, it wasn't easy. But, you know, I can't complain. I feel very fortunate about the position and the confidence that I have now.

So you created a sense of demand by waiting to get the script right?

No, I don't think I created a sense of 'demand'. I just did what I had to do.

And you weren't in a financial or professional situation where you needed to work?

I don't consider myself an ambitious guy and I can live very easily without much. So I was not looking for the opportunity to work on a big-budget film with big stars. That wasn't my objective. My objective was to make a good film with great actors whom

I respected. So in the moment that I showed them a good script with a great cast attached, and with the plan already completed, I think that it was a pretty attractive package for some studios.

How long had you been working on the screenplay at that point?

Almost two and a half years.

Have you received any negative responses from the press or colleagues in Mexico for not making your follow-up to Amores Perros *there?*

I feel like a Mexican rock'n'roll band on tour. I think of it as a Mexican film being shot in English. It's a Mexican screenwriter, a Mexican DP, a Mexican director, a Mexican production designer, a Mexican sound designer and an Argentinian musician. But there is also a Puerto Rican actor, an Australian actress, a French actress and an English actor, so the only main American character is really Sean Penn, alongside other great American actors in secondary roles. It can be considered a global film, but who cares? Is that important? I hate that stupid narrow way of thinking about nationalities within art. Art is universal.

Even having said this, when the film is released in Mexico there will be some criticism, and it's funny because when a soccer player goes to Europe to play everyone applauds him, or when a writer or a painter does the same, they learn and expand their perspective on their work. My question is: if a Mexican chef goes to New York and cooks his famous *huevos rancheros* using nothing but the finest of ingredients, including olive oil from Italy, eggs from Australia and chilli from India, are the *huevos rancheros* Mexican or American or are they eggs of the chef? Does a Mexican soccer player who's playing in the Spanish league lose his Mexican-ness? When John Huston came to Mexico to shoot, was he making a Mexican film or an American film? Or is it just a film? Was Chagal making French art because he was using French paint and painting in Paris or was he still a Russian paintor exploring other possibilities and speaking a universal language? Does where you shoot or how you shoot determine the nationality of a film? Is that important for the art? I don't give a damn.

That's true. It's not like anyone criticised Hemingway and F. Scott Fitzgerald for writing about their time in Paris in the 1920s.

That's just the thing. They spent that time there and it made their writing better because their perceptions changed. It's the same with directors.

Both Hemingway and Fitzgerald returned to America to live and work. Do you think you'll go back to Mexico and make films there?

Yes, I would like to shoot another film in Mexico very soon. I don't know if it will be the next one, but I hope to have another opportunity to make a film there because I have such a great time working there. As a fish, that's the soup where I belong.

Can you take me through the casting process? There are some very inspired choices there between Sean Penn, Benicio Del Toro and Naomi Watts.

When I had the idea to make a film in America, I already had Sean Penn in mind. He has always been one of my favorite actors. Not only is he one of the best actors in the world, but he also has a lot of integrity – which is very hard to find these days in this industry. He loves *Amores Perros* and we became friends when he called me at my home in Mexico City before I moved to LA. He was very generous about the film, telling me about how much *Amores Perros* meant to him. I was blown away to get this call, especially when I was already thinking of him for my next project. So I had him in mind for a long time. The only doubt I had about Sean is that for the character he plays, Paul, he has to be a very warm and sweet person, someone you have to love. Normally Sean plays the Jack role, so that was my only doubt. But then I thought, 'Come on, this is one of the best actors in the world, he can do anything he wants.' If he wants to be a dog, he can play a dog. He played the part of the sweet, vulnerable guy very well. I'll never forget that when Sean got the script he called me twenty minutes later and he said, 'This is an amazing script. What's going to happen? Tell me, are the kids going to die?' I just said, 'Read it.' Twenty minutes later he called me again and said, 'Come on, tell me, what's going to happen!' He was so excited, like a little kid, so that made me very happy. An hour later he called me and said, 'I'm in. This could be a masterpiece if it's well done. I want to go there.' Having Sean on the set is like playing soccer with Beckham.

With Benicio, I had also admired his work for some time. He has one of the most enigmatic faces. His eyes are very spiritual. He's a cinematic animal, mysterious. He's like a panther. By doing nothing, he can portray a lot of different things going on inside him. Benicio has an immense interior life and it shows in his eyes, and that's what differentiates a good actor from an extraordinary actor like him. He had a lot of offers after *Traffic*, but he turned them down and chose to do this film instead. He knew it was not a big-budget film and that he would have to make some sacrifices, but he did it anyway and I really appreciated that.

After I saw *Mulholland Drive*, I was blown away by Naomi Watts's range and then I saw a film called *Ellie Parker* that she and a friend did, and that was it! What I needed from Cristina was somebody who could go from a sweet woman to a woman with a desire for revenge. She is the Gena Rowlands of my generation: as fragile as a crystal but as strong as a diamond at the same time. You can't get any better that that. So I went to her trailer and I said, 'Hey, I want to offer you this part.' She didn't know what I was talking about and she accepted the role without having read it.

You went to see her on a movie set?

She was shooting another film, so I visited and knocked on the door of her trailer and said, 'Give me five minutes. I'm Alejandro González Iñárritu and I want to do my next film with you.' She said, 'What's it about?' I said, 'I cannot tell you, I don't have a script yet.' But she accepted my offer and she trusted me. The way all of those guys believed in me really meant something to me.

They must have thought you were telling the truth.

It's like how you have to trust your pilot. They believed that I would take them somewhere safely. The only thing is that you don't want to disappoint them with the result.

Were you at all intimidated, shooting this film in English in an American culture?

Having to speak in English for fourteen to sixteen hours a day meant that I had to translate from Spanish in my head and this is very hard for me because it meant that my brain had to work double, causing me to have headaches. It took me a while to understand the system. Who is who? Who is full of bullshit? Who is bluffing? Not to mention the bureaucracy and all of the things about the industry that I wasn't used to. It created a lot of stress because my English was limited. I had to use my hands and my face to make all kinds of communicative gestures to make the actors understand what I wanted. The main thing was that I trusted my actors. If they thought that a line would sound better in a different way, then we would try it. After all, it's their language.

By having them try different takes, you could figure out which line was the most truthful?

You can just hear it.

Was your editor Mexican?

No, he's American. It's the first time I've worked with him and, in fact, it's the first time I've worked with an editor because I always edit on my own, working alongside collaborators. He's amazing. His name is Stephen Mirrione and he won an Oscar for *Traffic*. He's smart, with great taste and patience. He is truly a great editor.

He must have relished the challenges the intricate structure of the film provides.

It was a good challenge. I took out many scenes, maybe twenty. Every time I took out a scene there was a domino effect, so I had to be very conscious each time, not only for the character and for the story of that character, but also to keep the balance of the story together.

You have said before that Memphis, where 21 Grams is shot, is very similar to Mexico City. Why do you think that?

I didn't want to shoot in New York or LA. I have seen so many films in those places that they have become like a set. So I began to travel with my DP, Rodrigo Prieto, and we looked around at some cities. What I like about Memphis is that it is like a Latin American city in a first-world country. As a Latin American I found that very interesting. It's a very abandoned city in some ways. It's not like it is here in LA where everyone is talking about money. It felt that it was more like a Mexican city. The people are more aware of their existence and real things. There is a kind of melancholy and nostalgia there. There's a history and uniqueness there. That's why the blues came from there; you can hear the blues in the weather, in the gardens and the texture of the buildings. You don't have that kind of pretentious global advertising that you see in other major cities. Memphis is the heart of America. A lot of political and racial issues have been going on there and because of all that suffering, and the textures in the city, you get a feel for its strong personality; you can almost smell the walls. In that sense, it is like Cuba. The people are so nice, and to me it's Middle America, because you can find real American people there.

What about your visual strategy for the film? Amores Perros *had a lot of kinetic camera work in it.*

While many DPs are worried about the beautifulness and the boring aesthetics, Rodrigo always bets for the truth of the moment. Nobody can touch your heart with a camera like he does. And one of the reasons is that he operates the camera, literally, very close to his heart. Like a painter, he uses the camera as a brush. The hand-held camera work is something that I wanted to do again because I felt this story needed that immediacy and reality. The hand-held is subordinated by the story and the characters. It wasn't as fast as it was in *Amores Perros* because this story is more of an interior story. Rodrigo and I used different stocks for each character. We were trying to dramatise their moments through the materials we shot with. We used very normal stock, like Vision 500, which is very plain, when the moments were tranquil and relaxed. When the characters became more unbalanced and the story gets darker we added more grain to the stock so there are many different textures jumping around in the film.

Our production designer, Brigitte Broch, suggested using a color for each character. She's like a psychiatrist. She can tell the backstory of someone just by looking at his lighter or his suitcase. Subtly, she defines the character and their emotion through different palettes of color – blue, green, yellow – and that helps the film with dimension. With every object she puts in the set, she tells us something about the character.

How did the film's production go?

It was very hard. I was a producer on the film and I discovered that the prices in America are three or four times what they are in Mexico. They were insulting. There are so many unions and so many rules here in America that you have to really understand the system to shoot here. So that was very frustrating for me. There's a rule of thumb in cinema: you never have enough money for any film, no matter if the budget is $500,000 or $200,000,000. Normally, the schedule often becomes very tight. To make things more difficult, I had to say goodbye to my producer two weeks before we started shooting because we did not understand each other. Then a week later I had to get rid of my Assistant Director, so the start was very complicated.

What happened with your producer?

I prefer not to discuss that because I don't want to hurt anyone. The relationship between directors and producers has always been conflicted since the beginning of cinema. I think it's because when you have a clear and strong vision about what you want, it's very hard to find someone who shares that. It's as hard as finding a husband or a wife and, in my situation, it was more difficult because I've always produced everything I've directed. In the end, he became the executive producer.

Getting back to the character of Paul . . . when you and Guillermo were going through the writing process, how did you, as a director, justify Paul's voice-over narration at the beginning and end of the film when neither Jack nor Cristina are given one?

Originally, the three characters each had their own introductory scene at the beginning of the film. Naomi, with a long therapy session in which she explained a little bit of her past and her struggles with the present; Benicio, as it is now, in the scene with the kid; and Sean with his voice-over. At the end, I cut almost all of the therapy scene with Cristina because I didn't consider it necessary now, and that's why I think it seems imbalanced. But now looking at it, I like it because with three different styles the audience is introduced to these characters in different ways. I think that if he's talking at the end of the film, it gives you a sense of his point of view of the story, as he remembered it and as he lies there dying.

He makes a sacrifice of himself, but would you call him a hero?

I hate the word 'hero'. What American people call heroes I call victims. Like the people who died in the World Trade Center – those people were not heroes, they were victims. So are the soldiers fighting in Iraq; they are the victims of the circumstances of this crazy fucking world. We can call Paul a victim, but he seems to have the redemptive strength in the film. How this guy can receive life from such a tragedy and then just give it away again to redeem these two people, helping Cristina get rid of that negative feeling of saving herself from killing Jack. She has to accept it to survive. Paul also owes Jack his life because if it weren't for Jack killing Cristina's husband, Paul wouldn't be alive – so his sacrifice is very complicated.

Guillermo claims that he is not concerned with 'likeability' when it comes to his characters. How do you feel about that? Some of the characters in your films can do some pretty horrible things. I'm thinking of Octavio trying to take his brother's wife in Amores Perros, *or the way Jack flees the scene of a deadly accident.*

I never thought about it in those terms. That's why I laugh when people mention my religion in relation to my work. It's not about Catholic things. People tend to think about Catholics as saints, but what you are talking about is human behaviour. That's why Guillermo calls me the most devilish Catholic and I call him the closet priest. Something that I hate about some American films, especially recently, is that the characters are so one-dimensional, so very predictable and polite. People are not good or bad. We are just floating in an immense universe of circumstances.

Moving into post-production – you were a very successful DJ at a radio station in Mexico City. Can you tell me something about the music in the film? It is a very sparse score.

The composer, Gustavo Santolalla, is the master in setting up the tone of an emotion with just two notes. He's a guy that leaves the show outside and gets to the essence of the scene just by touching the right strings, and you can hear the soul of the actor or the elephant in the room. I always felt that a good film should have no music. When a film works by itself, music should be talking about something else, possibly the opposite thing, and the synthesis of these things should create an interesting result. I will say that 1+1=3. I think that a lot of directors use music to suggest emotion because they were unable to accomplish what the scene was meant to accomplish through the direction. So by music you can guide the audience. 'OK, now you have to be sad. Play the violins. OK, now you have to be laughing. Play the drums.' So I was trying to use as little music as possible, expressing it as a subtle emotion coming from the characters as if it were coming from the air. There were no electronic instruments, it was just Gustavo blowing into PVC tubes or using a harmonium made in 1918. All the instruments are acoustic and very earthy. He is amazing . . . pure heart.

Do you really think that 21 Grams *is a film of hope?*

Somewhere between a film about hope and a film about survival. Life goes on, and even in the toughest circumstances, you can still find a way to survive. What could be tougher than to lose your own child? I don't think there is a worse drama than that.

I have always felt that life is a sequence of losses. From the first day we arrive here we lose many things: our innocence, our hair, our youth, our friends, our faith. It could be anything and everything. Life is about death and how you react to that. The last thing you lose is life, that's the last thing to go. You've already lost your parents, you're losing your memory . . . little by little you are losing things. People deal differently with loss. This is a film about loss: loss of faith with Jack, loss of health with Paul and loss of family with Cristina – and how they survive those losses through hope and acceptance. At the end I think Jack finally understands himself. He doesn't need to shout in his church because he has accepted himself; he knows who he is. The three of them have a very complicated nature and if they don't understand it, they won't survive. I think to survive you have to have hope, even if it is just a small light in a very dark place. I hope the film will give the audience some sense of redemption after they see it. My goal was not to make a devastating and dark film about life. I am sometimes like that, but not all the time. I can have horrible days like that when I can see everything as being dark, but sometimes I get some light and hope. But to understand the light, you have to know the darkness.

Do you know what you are going to do for your next film? Are you going to work with Guillermo again?

I consider *21 Grams* to be the second part of a trilogy that I am interested in making, a trilogy of intersection, triptychs and coincidences. I would like to explore that. The first one happened in Mexico, the second one happened in the United States and the third one will be global. That's what we are planning. I don't know when it will be done . . . maybe next year, maybe in twenty years.

So you and Guillermo are working on that together?

We're talking about it. I hope it doesn't take another three years. [*Laughs.*]

You dedicated the film to your wife. Can you tell me something about that decision?

My wife and I lost a newborn baby of ours named Luciano, so some of the emotions that were explored in the film, Maria, my wife, and I already had gone through. It was an experience I had to survive.

How did you and your wife get through that experience?

Just by getting closer, by loving each other and curing ourselves, and by accepting that there are things that you cannot control. One day you open your eyes and you are alive and then one day you are old. Another day you close your eyes and you are dead. Who gave you that? We don't own that. I always feel that people, mostly here in the United States, don't want to talk about death or confront it. It is the only big reality that we have. That is the only fucking thing we know for sure about our lives. The other stuff no one knows about. Here in America they deny all of that, they want to be young for ever. They don't talk about it, allowing their kids to grow with it. When you're looking at a woman with surgical breasts, a surgical butt and a surgical face, that's exactly the image of death. I think if you confront or talk about death it makes you more conscious of life and able to enjoy it that much more. It's like the sensation you get when you go to a funeral. You are very sad, but at the same it is a contradictory feeling because you are thinking, 'I'm glad that wasn't me.' I think that if people were more aware of that contradiction, then their lives would have greater meaning. Being conscious of your own fragility and vulnerability can make you stronger. Don't be afraid of death, it's with us every day.

Culver City, California, July 2003

21 Grams

1. INT. CRISTINA'S ROOM — DAY

Male and female clothing is strewn around an upper-middle-class room, decorated in good taste. A leather jacket hangs draped over a chair and a lead-blue dress lies on the floor.

Cristina (thirty-four) – thin, soft-skinned – sleeps face down, naked, half-covered by the sheets, barely lit by the light coming through the window.

Beside her, Paul (forty-one) naked, strong features, piercing eyes and messy hair – sits on the edge of the mattress, smoking and staring sadly at her.

He barely runs his fingers over her back without taking his eyes off her. Cristina shifts position without waking up.

He sits up, brings his hand to his brow, rubs his forehead and remains pensive as he looks at her.

Fade out.

Enter titles:

21 GRAMS

2. INT. SODA FOUNTAIN — NIGHT

Fade in to a soda fountain with white walls and red booths. The walls are hung with images of their products: milk shakes, sodas, hamburgers.

Michael (thirty-seven) – dressed informally, with a pleasant, relaxed face – sits at a table with his daughters: Laura (five) and Katie (four). Both look very pampered.

Laura slurps her chocolate milk shake through a straw.

MICHAEL

Sweetie, don't slurp.

LAURA

Why?

MICHAEL

It sounds awful.

LAURA

Daddy! But the bottom's the yummiest part!

She slurps again. Michael shakes his head in mild disapproval.

MICHAEL

Hurry up: Mom's waiting for us.

Katie starts blowing into her straw, making bubbles.

KATIE

Look, Daddy, a volcano . . .

MICHAEL

Your volcano's very pretty, but finish up your milk shake so
we can go see Mommy . . .

*She stops blowing and laps up the spilled milk shake from the edge of
the glass. Her father smiles condescendingly.*

3. INT. REHAB ROOM — DAY

*A group of people sits in a circle in a typical drug and alcohol group-
therapy session.*

*In the group is Cristina, with an intense look in her eyes, who seems to
have been at war for a long time and is finally on the way to finding
peace. She talks before the group's attentive stare.*

CRISTINA

Last night I was watching *Cinderella* with my daughters
when suddenly Laura, the older one, asked me why
neither Cinderella nor Beauty nor Ariel had mothers and,
goddammit, she was right: there are no mothers in Disney-
land. And they know about their grandma, that I was a
motherless child, and they're scared to death that they'll
lose me and I don't know what to tell them because I'm
just as fucking afraid. (*A beat.*) Afraid of losing control,
of ending up in a hospital again, dying from an overdose.

She remains meditative for a few seconds. It is obvious that she is in pain, but will not cry.

> I missed my mother terribly and, damn, I was furious when the cancer swallowed her up . . . she left me when I needed her most. And now I look at my daughters and Michael, and they love me, and I love them, and I know I can't fail them, I just can't . . .

She remains silent. It seems as if she wants to say something else, but she just smiles painfully.

4. INT. RELIGIOUS CENTRE ROOM − DAY

Jack (thirty-five) is a strong, wiry man, with a closely shaven face and wolfish features. He wears blue jeans, a short-sleeved shirt.

The phrase 'Jesus loves you' is tattooed on his left forearm, on his right are a Chinese ideogram and runes, and there is a star on the back of his right hand. A small heart is tattooed on his neck.

He sits on a wooden chair in a room decorated only by a cheap reproduction of a Renaissance hunting scene. An old refrigerator stands in one of the corners.

Seated in front of him is a skinny, black-haired boy (seventeen), also tattooed. They play Jenga on a table.

Jack pulls out a piece, places it on top and the tower sways slightly.

> JACK
> Think which one you're going to pull out.

> BOY
> I always think, man . . .

> JACK
> No, you don't: they didn't lock you up this time because you're not eighteen yet, but the next time you're gonna get fucked. Your turn.

The boy pulls out a block and the tower collapses.

> See: you're not thinking.

The boy sits, analysing his defeat. Jack stands up, gets some orange juice from the refrigerator, pours two glasses and gives one to the boy.

Stealing might get you money, you can tap some cheerleader's ass and you can show off riding some pickle-coloured Thunderbird, but tell me: what the fuck are you gonna do if you shoot a pregnant woman or an old man? Huh? You know what'll happen? The guilt will suck you down to the bones.

He drinks from his glass and looks at the boy again, who listens, annoyed.

No, stealing cars isn't worth it, believing in Jesus is . . .

He points at his 'Jesus loves you' tattoo. He stands up and walks over to the window.

Come here.

The boy walks over to him. Jack points at a new, double-cabin, silver Ford Lobo parked in the working-class street that runs by the religious centre.

See that truck? . . . It's a beauty, isn't it?

BOY

Yeah, it's cool.

Jack pulls out a key chain and presses the alarm button. The truck's horn honks and the lights flash.

JACK

I won it at a Walmart raffle . . .

BOY

No shit?

JACK

No shit. But it wasn't luck – it was Jesus that wanted me to have that truck

BOY
(*mocking*)

That's bullshit. I bet you stole it.

JACK

Jesus Christ gave it to me, it's he who gives and takes away.

BOY

Yeah right. He doesn't give a shit about us . . . I bet he doesn't even know I exist.

JACK

God even knows when a single hair moves on your head . . .

Jack presses the alarm button. The truck honks and flashes again.

5. INT. INTENSIVE CARE UNIT — DAY

Paul – with a grown beard, slightly long hair, and wearing a white robe – is half-sitting on a bed in the intensive care unit of a modest clinic.

He is connected to a respirator, with an IV in his left arm and electrodes attached to his chest. A discontinuous green line jumps in a monitor.

PAUL
(*voice-over*)

So this is death's waiting room? These ridiculous tubes, these needles swelling my arms? . . .

He looks around. Like him, there are many gravely ill patients; most of them are already on the verge of death.

What am I doing in this pre-corpse club? What do I have to do with them?

He looks at a fat old woman whose breathing inflates and deflates a rubber balloon beside her.

With her and the cancerous tumours rotting her stomach . . .

He then turns to look at a young man with a bandaged head.

. . . or with him, who fell drunk out of a third-floor window?

He closes his eyes.

I don't know when anything began any more . . .

7

He opens his eyes.

> . . . or when it's going to end.

He turns to look at the patients.

> They say we all lose 21 grams at the exact moment of our death. Everyone: 21 grams . . . the weight of a stack of five nickels, the weight of a hummingbird, a chocolate bar . . .

He stares at an unconscious young woman (twenty-six).

> Who'll be the first to lose their 21 grams? She, in a coma . . .

Paul, stunned, watches the pre-death spectacle.

> . . . or me?.

6. INT. HIGHWAY MOTEL BATHROOM — DAY

Cristina, dressed in black shorts and a T-shirt, is in a messy motel bathroom. A bare bulb mottled with fly excrement hangs from the ceiling. We hear the sound of water continuously leaking into the toilet. There is a cracked mirror above the filthy sink. Cheap flowery curtains cover the shower stall.

She opens a backpack and takes out a small baggie filled with cocaine. She scoops some out with a bottlecap and snorts it. She sits on the toilet cover, swallows and brings her hands to her head.

7. INT. EXAMINING ROOM, GYNAECOLOGIST'S OFFICE — DAY

Mary (thirty-eight), with vigorous, sweet eyes, is lying on a gynaecologist's examining table, with her legs open on the stirrups. A gynaecologist examines her with a nurse beside him. He finishes and looks her in the eyes.

> GYNAECOLOGIST
> You can get dressed now.

8. INT. GYNAECOLOGIST'S OFFICE — DAY

Mary is sitting before the gynaecologist in a nicely decorated but not over-luxurious office. The doctor looks over some charts.

GYNAECOLOGIST
For how long have you been trying to get pregnant?

MARY
A year and a half. (*Worried.*) Is there something wrong?

The doctor looks at her and hesitates before answering.

GYNAECOLOGIST
I'm afraid so. Your uterus and fallopian tubes are severely
damaged. It looks like you had an infection that was not
taken care of. (*A beat.*) Hadn't this been detected before?

MARY
They'd mentioned something, but . . .

Mary looks troubled. She turns to look at the doctor.

Will I be able to have children?

GYNAECOLOGIST
We can try surgery, but the probabilities would still be slim.

*Mary lowers her head, dismayed. The doctor gets up and sits on the
edge of the desk.*

Excuse me for asking this, but it's absolutely necessary that
you tell me the truth: have you ever had an abortion?

Mary thinks her answer over and slowly assents.

MARY
Yes.

GYNAECOLOGIST
Any reason?

Mary remains pensive again.

MARY
I got pregnant when I'd already separated from my
husband and I thought that . . .

GYNAECOLOGIST
(*uncomfortable*)
I meant medical reasons.

9

Mary lowers her head, ashamed.

> MARY
> (*mumbling*)

My husband is dying.

> GYNAECOLOGIST

I'm sorry?

> MARY

Paul, my husband, he's dying and I want to have his baby.

Mary stares absently. The doctor sits down next to her.

> GYNAECOLOGIST

We can operate and hope you get pregnant in three or four months.

> MARY
> (*smiling with bitter irony*)

He's got one month left at most.

The doctor looks at her, speechless.

9. EXT. PATIO, RELIGIOUS CENTER — DAY

Jack and the boy signal each other goodbye in the religious centre's patio – it looks like an old primary school. The boy runs off to join a group of young men like him playing basketball.

Reverend John (forty-eight) – rosy, red-haired with long sideburns and no moustache, dressed in a sort of black mess jacket – walks up to Jack as he looks at the boy.

> JOHN

How'd it go?

Jack shakes his head as he watches the boy play.

> JACK

Not good. This kid's going to end up in jail.

> JOHN

Be patient; all it takes is one sheep in a thousand . . .

They walk towards the exit and reach the door. A fat man with long hair catches up with them. He slaps Jack on the back and they stop.

> FAT MAN
> (*to John*)
> Afternoon, Reverend . . . (*to Jack*) Hey, Wolf, are you still having your birthday party on Wednesday?

> JACK
> Yep, my place.

> FAT MAN
> Cool . . .

The fat man leaves. Jack and John walk outside.

10. EXT. RELIGIOUS CENTER STREET — CONTINUOUS

> JACK
> See you later.

> JOHN
> See you . . .

They shake hands. Jack walks towards his truck, deactivates the alarm with the remote control and gets in.

11. EXT. JACK'S HOUSE — DAY

Jack's Ford Lobo parks in front of a humble house: a cheap one-floor construction in a working-class neighbourhood.

Several children are playing on the sidewalk, among them Freddy (nine) and Gina (seven) – Jack's children. Marianne (twenty-nine), his wife – athletic, streetwise, with some class – watches her children while sitting in a white plastic chair.

Jack gets out of the car and Freddy runs towards him.

> FREDDY
> Daddy.

Jack picks him up and kisses him. Marianne walks up to him with Gina who, more reserved, hugs her father's legs.

MARIANNE

Hey, honey . . .

They kiss hello.

FREDDY

Dad, are we going to go buy a dog?

MARIANNE

Freddy, we agreed no dogs.

FREDDY

Why not? You said that if I got good grades you'd buy me
one . . .

MARIANNE

Your sister has asthma and dog hair is bad for her . . .

FREDDY

It's bad for her, not me . . . Get *me* a dog . . .

JACK

No, and that's the end of it.

FREDDY

Well, at least get me a hamster . . .

JACK

We'll see . . .

FREDDY

Promise, huh? . . .

*Jack strokes his head and walks towards the house with Marianne in
his arms.*

12. EXT. MOTEL SWIMMING POOL — DAY

*Paul is sitting on an old pool chair made of interlaced plastic strips.
His face is filthy with dust and sweat.*

*Absorbed, he stares at the empty pool, the bottom covered with
branches, dry leaves and dirt. Behind him are the rooms of a dusty
desert motel. Far off we can hear the coos of a mourning dove.*

Cristina (dressed as she was in Scene 6 where she snorts the cocaine) finds Paul and walks towards him. She stands in front of him. Paul lifts his hand to shield his eyes from the sun vibrating behind Cristina.

CRISTINA

Where were you?

Paul doesn't answer. He pulls a revolver from his waist, opens the cylinder and empties out three shells. He puts them on the glass top of a white, wrought-iron table. Mesmerised, Cristina examines one of them.

Did you kill him?

Paul nods. Cristina grows pale and runs her left hand through her hair. Both remain silent.

13. INT. PRISON HALLWAY — DAY

Jack walks down the hallway of a large jail, escorted by two guards. Many inmates mock him through the bars.

INMATE 1

What happened? Jesus don't love you no more?

INMATE 2

Hey, Wolf! You're back, motherfucker.

Jack pays no attention. His serious, concentrated stare contrasts with their babbling.

They reach a cell. One of the guards opens it and signals Jack to get inside.

GUARD 1

Welcome home, asshole.

Jack glares at him. He walks in and they slam the gate shut.

14. INT. INDOOR POOL — NIGHT

There are three or four people swimming leisurely in the pool. In the fourth lane, Cristina swims in at full speed. Down the third, several feet behind, comes her sister Claudia (twenty-seven). She is slender and looks like Cristina.

I win.

Claudia also takes off her cap and goggles.

CLAUDIA

You're just lucky.

Cristina splashes water in her eyes.

CRISTINA

Don't be a sore loser.

She smiles, confident. A cellphone starts ringing. Cristina lifts herself out of the pool. She walks towards a chair, grabs a towel, dries her hands and opens her gym bag.

When she pulls out the cellphone it stops ringing. She looks at the screen and puts it away. Claudia catches up with her and sits on the chair beside her.

CLAUDIA

Do you want to go to the jacuzzi for a while?

CRISTINA

I can't. Michael and the girls must be waiting for me already . . .

CLAUDIA

OK, I'll see you later.

Claudia walks towards one side of the pool. Cristina wraps herself up in a towel and grabs her gym bag. When she is about to go, Claudia calls out to her.

Cristina . . .

Cristina turns around.

15. INT. MEETING HALL, RELIGIOUS CENTER — AFTERNOON

Men and women who look like sinners being saved are taking part in a religious ceremony led by John. Among them are Jack and his family, dressed as they were in Scene 11 when Jack gets home.

There is no religious imagery inside the hall. There are no pews, only twelve metal chairs against the walls, where two or three old women sit.

They all repeat John's words in unison.

>   JOHN
> Jesus is our hope . . .

>   EVERYONE
> Jesus is our hope . . .

>   JOHN
> Jesus is our light . . .

>   EVERYONE
> Jesus is our light . . .

>   JOHN
> Jesus is our forgiveness . . .

>   EVERYONE
> Jesus is our forgiveness . . .

>   JOHN
> Jesus is the water that quenches my thirst . . .

>   EVERYONE
> Jesus is the water that quenches my thirst . . .

Jack repeats the phrases passionately. Marianne, looking at him annoyed, barely mutters them.

16. INT. BEDROOM, PAUL'S APARTMENT — AFTERNOON

Paul is lying on his bed watching the news on TV in a well-furnished but unpretentious apartment. He looks very thin, some fifteen pounds underweight, ragged and pale.

He breathes oxygen through a tube connected to his nose from a green tank on wheels.

He sits up with difficulty and turns off the TV. He fixes his robe and stands up, taking care not to get tangled. He walks into the bathroom, trailing the tank behind him.

17. INT. BATHROOM, PAUL'S APARTMENT — DAY/EVENING

He locks the door. In front of the mirror are several photographs of babies and on the sink there is a rubber ducky. Paul looks at it and puts it back in its place.

He bends down and opens the cabinet under the sink. He rummages around rolls of toilet paper, soap, shampoo, until he finds a small plastic tube. He opens it and sits on the toilet.

Inside there is a cigarette and a lighter. Paul takes the tubing out of his nose and lights the cigarette. He breathes in deeply and exhales the smoke with great pleasure.

Noises. Paul pricks up his ear. He gives the cigarette a long drag, opens the window and flicks it out.

> MARY
> (*out of shot*)
>
> Hey baby, I'm home . . .

He tries to push the smoke out of the window with his hands.

18. INT. LIVING ROOM, PAUL'S APARTMENT — CONTINUOUS

Mary (dressed as she was in Scene 8 where she saw the gynaecologist) sets a briefcase and some papers down on the living-room table.

> PAUL
> (*out of shot*)
>
> Hi.

Mary jumps, startled.

> MARY
>
> Jesus, you scared me.

Paul smiles, breathing agitatedly from the effort in getting there. She moves close to kiss him.

> How are you feeling?

> PAUL
> (*ironic*)
>
> Just great . . .

Mary does not find the answer funny. She notices something on him and draws close to smell him.

> MARY
> Have you been smoking again?

Paul shrugs his shoulders. She gets upset.

> For fuck's sake, Paul. If they find out you're smoking
> they're going to take you off the transplant list. Don't you
> get it?

Paul puffs, unaffected. Mary starts to search under one of the sofa's cushions and can't find anything. She goes over to a different couch and finds a plastic tube like the one Paul opened in the bathroom.

> PAUL
> If I don't smoke I'll go nuts. I'm sick of being locked up in
> here.

> MARY
> Better nuts than dead.

Mary breaks the cigarette into pieces and turns to him.

> I don't know how the hell you get them.

19. INT. PRISON HALLWAY — DAY

All the cells are empty with their doors open except for Jack's. He sits on his cot, inert.

The head guard walks by the cell and turns to one of his subordinates.

> HEAD GUARD
> He still won't come out to eat?

> GUARD
> He's been on water for three days now. Do I bring him
> something?

> HEAD GUARD
> No, let the fucker starve.

20. INT. MOTEL ROOM — NIGHT/DAWN

Paul is lying on a motel-room floor (the same as where Cristina snorted the coke in Scene 6), with a gunshot wound in his chest. He is barefoot, with his soles bleeding among the broken shards of glass. His shirt is soaked in blood.

Cristina is bent over him, trying to rouse him. She turns to Jack, who is standing at one end of the room with his forearm torn and covered in clotting blood, his face and body beaten.

CRISTINA

Call an ambulance.

Jack remains motionless, stunned.

(*screaming*) Call an ambulance, goddammit.

Jack is motionless for a few more seconds. Seeing that Jack does nothing, Cristina grabs Paul by the underarms and starts to drag him out of the room, leaving a thick trail of blood on the floor.

Jack seems to snap out of his stupefaction and runs to help her.

21. EXT. MOTEL PARKING LOT — CONTINUOUS

Jack and Cristina carry Paul out, bleeding.

22. EXT. CRISTINA'S HOUSE — DAY

Paul is standing outside Cristina's house in an upper-middle-class residential area. He rings the doorbell repeatedly, but no one opens.

He takes two steps back, stares at the entire house and leaves.

23. EXT. GOLF COURSE — DAY

Several caddies are chatting, sitting on parked golf carts at the edge of the golf course.

Jack arrives carrying a golf bag. He is dressed in white like the others, but wears a long-sleeve shirt.

Jack drops the bag heavily next to one of the carts. One of the caddies makes fun of him.

CADDY 1
What's the matter? Sticks too heavy for you?

Jack smiles and grabs his crotch.

JACK
Just this one. Wanna help me carry it?

The answer makes the other caddies cackle. One of them points to a cooler overflowing with beers.

CADDY 2
Have a cold one.

He walks over to the cooler, rummages under the beers and pulls out a coke. He lifts it up, shows it and toasts alone.

Another caddy walks over to the cooler, takes a beer, opens the can and raises it.

CADDY 3
To all the holes in the world.

Al (fifty), a robust man, walks over to them.

Hey, Al, want a beer?

He vehemently refuses, shaking his head. He walks towards Jack and stands in front of him.

AL
The boss wants to talk to you.

24. INT. HEAD OF CADDIES' OFFICE — DAY

Jack is sitting before Brown (forty), the head of caddies. He is wearing thick glasses, a cheap tie and a blue shirt with sweat stains around the armpits.

JACK
(*upset*)
I know I'm not a caddy yet, but I'm working at it. I'm learning, Brown, I swear, I won't make you look bad . . .

BROWN

That's not the problem, Jack. The thing is, some members have been complaining about your tattoos.

Jack shows him his shirtsleeve.

JACK

I've got a long-sleeve shirt; you can't see them.

Brown gets up and points to a tattoo on Jack's neck.

JACK

What about that one? Does your sleeve cover that one too, or are you going to start wearing a scarf?

Brown looks out of the window and points to some golf players.

Look, Jack, this is a club for people different from you and me, you understand, right?

Jack looks hurt.

JACK

Brown, I don't drink, I don't steal, I'm clean; why are you firing me?

BROWN

I know you're clean; that's why I hired you. But this decision comes from the administration and if I don't follow through they'll fuck me too. (*A beat.*) I got you a hefty severance cheque. You can pick it up at the cashier.

Jack looks shocked. He runs his fingers through his hair and stands up, apparently calm. Brown holds out his hand; Jack just looks at him scornfully.

Try to understand.

Suddenly, Jack gets a putter from a bag in the corner and feigns he is about to smash some paintings of old-fashioned golfers.

Brown stands fearless, waiting for him to finish releasing his anger. Jack doesn't break the paintings, throws the putter away and leaves, slamming the glass door behind him. Luckily, it does not break.

25. INT. LAUNDRY ROOM, CRISTINA'S HOUSE — DAY

Cristina is sitting alone in front of the washing machine. She smokes nervously with teary eyes and drinks repeatedly from a bottle of vodka. On the washing machine are two black bags.

She grabs one of the bags, sighs deeply and opens it. She pulls out a bloodied girl's dress, the same Katie was wearing in Scene 2. She spreads it out, looks at it painfully, then puts it into the washing machine.

She keeps pulling out Katie's clothes and with each one Cristina seems to break down, but does not cry. The phone starts ringing, but she pays no attention.

Finally, she pulls out a pair of blue sneakers with red shoelaces. She looks at them for a long time. She puts them to one side and covers her face with her left hand. The phone will not stop ringing.

26. EXT. HUMUS-PROCESSING PLANT — DAY

In a large humus-processing plant in the middle of the desert, Jack shovels black earth and puts it in a sack. Black dust covers the scene and Jack looks dirty.

Several workers shovel around Jack without noticing him.

27. INT. HOSPITAL ROOM — AFTERNOON

Paul is lying on a bed with his torso uncovered. There is an enormous scar running down his chest.

Doctor Rothberg (fifty) – robust, red-haired – examines him. Beside him is Dolores (sixty), the nurse, a woman with deep-blue eyes, plump, maternal.

ROTHBERG

Is there any pain?

PAUL

My head aches.

ROTHBERG

That's normal; your blood pressure's low. We're going to give you a shot to make you feel better.

Dolores pulls out a syringe and prepares the injection.

I brought what you asked for.

From a suitcase, he pulls out a glass jar in which floats a human heart. Bewildered, Paul looks at the jar.

PAUL

Is that my heart?

Rothberg nods and hands it to him. Paul stares at it, speechless. He shakes the jar. The heart sways slowly in the jar, bouncing against the glass walls.

28. INT. PAUL'S CAR, HUMUS-PROCESSING PLANT — DAY

Paul and Cristina drive down a road by the side of the vast desert. In the distance are several parked trucks. Several workers, Jack among them, load the truck with the sacks of humus.

CRISTINA

Which one is he?

PAUL

The one in the white shirt.

Cristina watches Jack as the car moves on.

29. EXT. HIGHWAY'S EDGE — CONTINUOUS

Jack sees Paul's car drive by and his eyes meet with Cristina's, who stares at him fiercely. He sees them drive on, grabs a sack and loads it into the truck.

30. INT. PAUL'S CAR, DESERT — CONTINUOUS

Paul accelerates past the trucks. Cristina breathes through her mouth, nervously.

PAUL

Are you OK?

She turns to look at him fixedly. She can barely speak.

CRISTINA

I'm going to kill him . . . I'm going to kill him.

Paul moves forward some more. He stops the car, embraces Cristina and caresses her tenderly. She receives his caresses, breathing agitatedly.

(*Whispering.*) We have to kill him . . . please . . .

31. INT. JACK'S HOUSE — DAY

Jack's house is humble. The living room is sparsely furnished, decorated with cheap Walmart paintings — vases, boats — all surrounding a large colour photograph of Jack and his family receiving the keys to the Ford Lobo in front of a Walmart.

A broken electric fan sits in one of the corners. In the centre stands an old television set — one of the first made with a remote control.

Jack and his family are sitting in the dining room, holding hands while he says grace.

JACK

Thank you, Lord, for keeping us together, for filling us with love and for giving us this meal. Amen.

EVERYONE

Amen.

They let go of their hands and Marianne starts serving.

JACK
(*to Marianne*)

I got fired from the club.

Marianne holds the serving spoon in mid-air.

MARIANNE

The usual?

The children start fighting.

GINA

Stop grabbing my bread.

JACK
(*to Marianne*)

I guess so.

MARIANNE

Now what are we going to do?

JACK

I'll find something.

The children keep fighting. Suddenly Freddy hits Gina in the arm.
She complains immediately.

GINA

Mommy, Freddy hit me in the arm.

MARIANNE

Freddy, stop it.

GINA

Mom, it hurts.

Jack drops his fork and knife on the table, annoyed.

JACK

Which arm?

GINA

This one.

JACK

Hold out your other arm.

MARIANNE

Jack, don't start.

JACK

Hold it out and let your brother hit you.

MARIANNE

Jack, no.

JACK
(*to Marianne*)
'Whoever hits you on your right cheek, turn the other to
him also.' (*to the girl, who hesitates*) Hold it out.

She obeys and holds out her arm.

(*to Freddy*) Hit her.

The boy hesitates.

I said hit her.

*The boy hits her and Gina screams in pain. Marianne pushes her
chair out and stands up, angry. She walks towards her daughter, grabs
her by the hand and takes her away.*

*Freddy is scared. Jack stares at him and slaps him violently on the
nape of the neck.*

There's no hitting in this house.

He slaps him again.

Understood?

He turns to keep eating his spaghetti.

32. INT. PAUL'S BEDROOM – NIGHT

*Paul is lying in bed, connected to the oxygen tank. He is reading a
magazine by his bedside lamp. Mary, with her back turned to him,
undresses.*

*Mary slips on a nightgown and sits down in front of the mirror to
comb her hair. She puts the brush down and turns to Paul.*

MARY
Next Friday, ask Lupe to stay the night. I can't stay because
I invited the company managers over for dinner.

PAUL
I fired Lupe.

MARY
You fired her? Why?

PAUL

She made me feel like a cripple.

MARY

Goddammit, Paul, now who's going to cook for you? Who's going to clean up after you? Who's going to take care of you? Who?

PAUL

I can do it by myself.

Mary shuts her eyes, annoyed.

MARY

I can't any more, Paul. Really, I can't.

Mary brings her hand to her forehead and rubs it, hurt. He gets up with difficulties and walks towards her. She sits down next to him and he hugs her. She stays still.

After a while, playfully, Paul starts kissing her neck. He pulls down her bra and strokes her breast.

What are you doing?

PAUL

What does it feel like?

She pulls his hand away.

MARY

You might hurt yourself. Besides, I need you to . . .

She is silent for a few moments, pensive. She grabs his hand and looks him in the eye.

I went to a fertility clinic.

Paul sighs in disapproval.

PAUL

More doctors? Mary, we've talked about this . . .

MARY

No, this is a specialist. He said that with surgery I might get pregnant in three months. You need to donate sperm and then . . .

Paul lets go of her hand and stands up.

PAUL

Mary: no.

MARY

I could take care of him . . .

PAUL

But I can't. No, Mary, no. What's the point?

They are silent. Mary holds out her hand and grabs Paul's. She pulls it towards her.

MARY

It's what I most want in the world. Do it for me, please.

PAUL

Why do you want my child? I'm dying.

MARY

Please.

Paul puts his hand on his brow and doesn't say anything else.

33. EXT. CRISTINA'S HOUSE – DAY

Paul is parked in front of Cristina's house, watching. It is hot; Paul sweats. She does not appear. He gets out of the car and wipes the sweat from his forehead.

Cristina walks out when he is slightly distracted. She strolls down the sidewalk past Lucio (twenty) – a skinny Salvadorian boy who is tending a garden.

LUCIO

Morning, ma'am.

CRISTINA

Good morning, Lucio.

Paul watches Cristina walk down the street.

34. EXT. STREET — CONTINUOUS

Paul follows her discreetly a few yards away. She walks into a convenience store. Paul follows.

35. INT. CONVENIENCE STORE — CONTINUOUS

She grabs some yogurts from the refrigerator, then browses the aisles and grabs a bottle of vodka. Paul watches her carefully.

Cristina heads over to the cashier to pay. Paul grabs a box of Frosted Flakes and lines up behind her. He does not stop scrutinising her: the nape of her neck, her back, her hair, her hands.

It is Cristina's turn. The cashier rings up the items.

> CASHIER
> Did you find everything you needed today, ma'am?

Cristina nods.

> That'll be twenty-three dollars and eighteen cents.

Cristina pays, takes her yogurts and leaves. Paul watches her go.

> (*to Paul*) Did you find everything you needed today, sir?

36. EXT. STREET — MOMENTS LATER

Paul walks out with his shopping bag. He sees Cristina walk away. He pulls out a cigarette, lights it and watches her get lost in the distance.

37. EXT. LIVING ROOM JACK'S HOUSE — NIGHT

Marianne is in her living room surrounded by several guests: ex-convicts (among them the fat man from Scene 9), door-to-door salesmen, converted young men, women with dyed hair and Reverend John.

On the tables are bottles of soda, potato chips, pretzels, but no alcohol. The only smoker in the room is a squalid, pale young woman.

The house seems too small for so many guests, and Marianne seems uncomfortable. She moves from one group of people to the next almost without talking to anyone. Overwhelmed, Marianne goes to the kitchen.

38. INT. KITCHEN — CONTINUOUS

Three people chat inside. In front of the stove, Trish (forty) slim, wearing jeans and a black T-shirt – is stirring soup in a large pot. She turns towards Marianne.

> TRISH
> It's ready.

Marianne grabs a spoon and tastes it.

> When does my brother plan to show up?

> MARIANNE
> He said he'd be back by eight.

The others leave the kitchen; only Trish and Marianne remain. Trish looks around her and checks that no one is watching. She ducks down and pulls out an open beer from under the sink. She shows it to Marianne.

> TRISH
> One hundred per cent pure Corona.

She gives it to Marianne, who turns her back to the door. She takes a gulp and looks disgusted.

> MARIANNE
> It's warm.

> TRISH
> You wanna spend the night drinking lemonade?

Marianne smiles in complicity, feigns giving the beer back and then gives it another drink. Both break into laughter.

39. INT. HALL CRISTINA'S HOUSE — NIGHT

Cristina walks in with a gym bag. She is wearing sweatpants and her hair is wet. The house is cosy, with family portraits of Michael, the children and herself. Brick walls, several plants. She stops at the foot of the stairs.

> CRISTINA
> I'm home . . .

Nobody answers. She puts the bag down and walks up the stairs.

40. INT. HALL CRISTINA'S HOUSE – CONTINUOUS

She walks down the hall. She listens for voices: nothing.

> CRISTINA
> Katie, Laura, where are you?

She opens a door and we can see the girls' room.

41. INT. GIRLS' ROOM CRISTINA'S HOUSE – CONTINUOUS

She walks into the room and turns her cellphone on to listen to her messages. While she does so she starts picking up after her daughters and tidying the room up.

> FATHER
> (*out of shot*)
> Sweetie, I was just calling to see if you wanted to have lunch next week . . . call me . . .

She presses a button to listen to the next message.

> MICHAEL
> (*out of shot*)
> Hey, honey, we're on our way home. If you need me to pick up anything on the way, give me a call on my cellphone.

She walks around the room fixing things as she listens. She stops to rearrange some dolls. On the cellphone, voices are heard.

> LAURA
> (*out of shot*)
> Daddy, Daddy . . . a kitty . . .

> MICHAEL
> (*out of shot*)
> Don't touch it . . . Laura, leave it . . . OK, honey, I'll see you at home.

Cristina presses a few buttons, hangs up and leaves the room.

42. INT. KITCHEN CRISTINA'S HOUSE — CONTINUOUS

She walks into the kitchen. She opens the sports bag, pulls out the towel and swimsuit (the ones used in Scene 14) and drapes them over a chair.

She opens the pantry and takes out four plates. She starts setting up four places for dinner on the kitchen table.

The phone rings. Cristina answers while she arranges the plates.

> CRISTINA
> Hello . . . speaking . . .

As she listens, the expression on her face changes.

> What . . . ? Where?

43. INT. REVEREND JOHN'S CAR — NIGHT

John drives an old 1983 Pontiac. Marianne sits beside him. Both are silent and slightly uncomfortable.

In the distance we see a group of curious onlookers lit intermittently by a patrol-car turret.

They slowly drive past the scene. Nothing can be seen between the group of onlookers. A girl's shoe lies a few feet ahead.

John parks the car further on and opens the door.

> JOHN
> Stay here, I'll be right back.

He gets out. Marianne stays in the car, breathing nervously.

44. INT. DOCTOR'S OFFICE — AFTERNOON

Paul, looking terrible, sits in a wheelchair and is connected to a small oxygen tank. He is next to Mary, before the gynaecologist.

> GYNAECOLOGIST
> Are you sure you want to do this?

                    MARY
              (*answering quickly*)
We're sure.

                GYNAECOLOGIST
Even if the operation is successful, artificial insemination
doesn't always work.

                    MARY
It doesn't matter, we want to try.

The doctor points at a door and turns to Paul.

                GYNAECOLOGIST
Please come this way.

Mary gives Paul a kiss. He heads for the door in his wheelchair.

45. INT. CUBICLE — MOMENTS LATER

Paul wheels himself in. The doctor looks at him seriously.

                GYNAECOLOGIST
This is about having a child, Paul. And . . . with your
condition . . . you know you probably won't ever meet him.

                    PAUL
Life must go on, right?

*The gynaecologist sighs in disapproval. He opens a drawer and pulls
out a plastic receptacle and a latex glove and gives them to him.*

                GYNAECOLOGIST
You need to put this glove on to avoid contaminating the
sample. Make sure it all lands in the receptacle.

From a cabinet, he pulls out a Playboy *and gives it to Paul.*

In case you need some inspiration.

*The doctor smiles mischievously and walks out. Paul seems
embarrassed by the situation. He unzips his pants and leafs through
the magazine.*

Cristina walks into the hospital and hurries towards the front desk. She stands before the receptionist.

CRISTINA

My husband and daughters were in an accident and I was told to come here.

RECEPTIONIST

What are their names?

CRISTINA

Michael, Katherine and Laura Beck.

Cristina is nervous and impatient. The woman types on the computer and looks at the monitor for a moment. She turns towards Cristina hesitantly.

RECEPTIONIST

Excuse me for a minute.

She heads towards an office with translucent glass walls. Point of view of Cristina, watching her calling someone on the phone.

Cristina's father (sixty-five) – tall, bearded, with grey hair and a withered face slightly resembling Cristina's – arrives with Claudia. Cristina hugs her father.

FATHER

What happened?

CRISTINA

I don't know, they haven't told me.

Claudia walks over to her and strokes her hair.

CLAUDIA

It's going to be alright.

The receptionist returns.

RECEPTIONIST

The head surgeon, Doctor Jones, will be with you in a moment. Please wait for him in the waiting room on the fourth floor.

Cristina grabs her by the arm rather violently.

> CRISTINA
>
> What happened to my family?

The woman looks at her, frightened. She points at the waiting room.

> RECEPTIONIST
>
> Please wait for Doctor Jones.

Cristina tries to say something else, but her father pulls her away by the elbow and takes her to the waiting room.

47. INT. LIVING ROOM JACK'S HOUSE – NIGHT

The guests mill around the living room. The fat man, surrounded by a small group, tells a joke that Marianne listens to leaning against the kitchen door frame.

> FAT MAN
>
> Do you know what the most important question for safe sex is? (*A beat.*) What time does your husband get home?

Several guests cackle at the joke. Marianne laughs discreetly. The noise of a car is heard and Marianne turns towards the kitchen.

48. INT. KITCHEN JACK'S HOUSE – CONTINUOUS

Trish peers out of the window and sees Jack's Ford Lobo pull up.

> TRISH
>
> His Highness has arrived.

Marianne stands next to Trish and also peers out.

> MARIANNE
>
> Let's see what he comes up with.

She moves away from the window, walks towards the stove, lights one of the burners and puts a frying pan on the fire.

> What's he doing?

> TRISH
>
> I don't know, he's just sitting there.

Marianne walks towards the door that leads outside.

> MARIANNE
> (*to Trish*)
>
> Don't let the rice burn.

49. EXT. DRIVEWAY JACK'S HOUSE — CONTINUOUS

*The truck still has its headlights on. Marianne knocks on the window.
Jack lowers it; he looks crushed.*

> MARIANNE
>
> It's eight o'clock. What are you going to make up now?
> Traffic? Or were you 'preaching the Word' when the entire
> congregation has been here waiting for you for the past two
> hours? It's your party, remember?

*He keeps his eyes on the dashboard and does not answer. Marianne
leans towards him, irritated.*

> What's wrong with you? Have you been drinking?

Jack shakes his head. Marianne draws close to him.

> Did you drink again?

Jack swallows and starts to speak quietly.

> JACK
>
> I ran over a man and two girls.

> MARIANNE
> (*stunned*)
>
> You're lying, right?

> JACK
>
> I was speeding home to make it to dinner, and I turned too
> quickly and they were crossing the street and . . .

*Jack chokes up and cannot go on. She walks towards the hood; it is
dented and bloodstained.*

*With her right index finger, Marianne touches the blood and lifts it to
her eyes as if she wants to make sure it is real. She feels it with her
fingers and, horrified, turns to look at Jack, who can barely be seen in
the darkness.*

50. INT. PAUL'S CAR — NIGHT/DAWN

Jack drives nervously. Every time a trailer or truck drives by him, he jerks the steering wheel.

Cristina sits in the back seat. Paul's head is on her lap; his chest is covered in blood. She strokes his forehead repeatedly.

51. INT. POST-OP ROOM HOSPITAL — EVENING

Paul is sitting down, his torso bare, connected to several electrodes.

Rothberg and Dolores are in front of him. Mary holds his hand.

> ROTHBERG
>
> Deep breath . . .

Paul acts accordingly. Rothberg looks at a monitor.

> Good. You're doing very well. Your lungs are clear.

Dolores walks over to him and starts removing the electrodes, while Rothberg writes something down in a notebook.

> PAUL
>
> My new heart, whose was it?

Rothberg stops writing and looks at him.

> ROTHBERG
>
> I can't tell you – hospital regulations. Just like the donor's family doesn't know your name either.

> PAUL
>
> I need to know, really.

> ROTHBERG
>
> It's not worth it. This is your heart now. That's all that should matter to you. OK?

> DOLORES
>
> If you want, you can write an anonymous letter to the family members through the donors' organisation.

Mary turns to look at him.

MARY

See? It's better that you don't know.

Paul turns to look at her harshly.

52. INT. WAITING ROOM — NIGHT

Cristina, her father and Claudia wait silently. Doctor Molina (fifty-two), still in his surgical gown, and Doctor Jones (sixty), who is wearing a white gown, slacks and a tie, walk up to them accompanied by a nurse (thirty-four).

As soon as they arrive, Cristina stands up.

DOCTOR JONES

Mrs Beck?

CRISTINA
(*anxious*)
What happened to my family?

With a gesture from his hand, Doctor Jones asks them to sit.

DOCTOR JONES

Your husband and daughters were hit by a car. We had to perform an emergency operation on your husband.

He turns to the other doctor.

DOCTOR MOLINA

Your husband suffered multiple skull fractures and we had to remove several blood clots in the brain. He is in a very critical condition and we're concerned that he doesn't have some of the brain reflexes.

Cristina is shocked by the news. She takes a deep breath.

CRISTINA

Is he going to be alright?

DOCTOR MOLINA

We're doing the best we can.

CRISTINA

What about my daughters?

The doctors look at each other. They are silent. Doctor Jones looks Cristina in the eyes.

> DOCTOR JONES
> Your youngest daughter was brought in with a severe haemorrhage. She just wasn't able to get here soon enough.

Doctor Jones finds it difficult to go on. Cristina's jaw starts shaking slightly. Doctor Jones seems to gain strength.

> They both died in the accident. I'm very sorry.

Cristina clenches her teeth and suddenly crumbles and starts to cry, holding her face in her hands.

> CRISTINA
> It's not true, no, no . . .

Her father does not know whether to hold her or look at her.

> No, no, no . . . where are my daughters? I want to see my girls.

> DOCTOR JONES
> The bodies are here. You can see them if you want, but I wouldn't recommend it . . .

The doctor's speech seems out of place and he stops mid-sentence.

> CRISTINA
> No, no, no . . .

> DOCTOR JONES
> I'm very sorry. (*to the father*) If you'll excuse us, we have to get back to Mr Beck.

The doctors get up and leave. They signal the nurse to stay.

Cristina cannot stop crying. She holds on to her sister.

53. INT. LIVING ROOM JACK'S HOUSE – NIGHT

In the living room, the fat man starts to chant.

> FAT MAN
> WE – WANT – DIN – NER, WE – WANT – DIN – NER!

The other guests join in, John among them.

> EVERYONE
> WE – WANT – DIN – NER . . .

Trish looks at them from the kitchen door and then looks out again.

54. EXT. JACK'S HOUSE – NIGHT

Marianne is standing in front of the truck, which still has its lights on. Trish looks at them from the window and walks out.

> TRISH
> What happened?

Marianne stares at the moths fluttering around the truck's headlights.

> MARIANNE
> Jack ran over a man and some girls. He thinks he killed them.

> TRISH
> Oh God, no.

> MARIANNE
> Tell Reverend John to stay, make sure no one notices and get everyone to leave.

> TRISH
> But, what happened?

> MARIANNE
> Just do what I tell you to do.

55. INT. CAFETERIA SPORTS CLUB – AFTERNOON

Cristina limply floats face up in the pool. Paul watches her from a window in the cafeteria while drinking a glass of milk.

56. INT. INDOOR POOL – CONTINUOUS

Cristina gets out of the pool. She grabs a towel and dries herself off.

57. INT. CAFETERIA SPORTS CLUB — CONTINUOUS

Paul watches her closely.

58. INT. CADDIES' HOUSE GOLF CLUB — EVENING

Jack is standing in front of some lockers (dressed as he was in Scene 49, where he confesses the accident to Marianne). He removes his clothes and various objects and puts them in a duffle bag.

Caddy 1 is sitting on a bench, watching him.

> CADDY I
> I know the head of caddies at the Vista Real. I can set you up . . .

> JACK
> No thanks, man. I'll figure it out.

Jack closes his locker and walks over to the other caddy.

> Thanks for everything. I'll see you around.

The caddy stands up. They knock fists.

59. EXT. PARKING LOT — MOMENTS LATER

The sun starts to set. Several blackbirds fly towards some trees. Jack heads towards his truck.

He opens it and throws his bag inside. In the distance, Brown spots him and walks over.

> BROWN
> Hey . . .

Jack turns to look at him suspiciously.

> What are you doing here?

> JACK
> I came to get my things.

Jack moves to get into his truck. Brown leans on the door.

> BROWN

I didn't fire you, Jack. If it were up to me I never would've fired you . . .

Jack breathes in deeply and looks at him suspiciously.

> JACK

You swear to God you had nothing to do with this?

> BROWN

I don't believe in God . . .

> JACK

You should . . .

Brown loosens his tie. Jack still looks at him warily.

> BROWN

Come on, I'll buy you a beer.

> JACK

I don't drink any more.

Brown laughs and pats Jack on the back.

> BROWN

You should . . . come on, just a couple of beers. It's been a while since we talked.

Jack doesn't answer.

> Come on. I've been thinking of a job I can hook you up with. What do you say?

Jack thinks about it for a few seconds.

> JACK

OK, let's go.

60. INT. QUIET ROOM HOSPITAL – NIGHT

Two women (fifty) enter the waiting room. Liz – kind eyes, calm – approaches them. Cristina is being consoled, sitting between her father and Claudia.

LIZ

Ma'am . . .

The three look up. The women sit on the chairs in front of them. They look at the women expectantly.

Mrs Beck, I'm very sorry for your loss. As you know, the doctors did everything they could to save your husband's life, but he has shown no brain activity . . .

Liz breathes in. It looks like she is about to say something but doesn't dare to. Cristina cannot stop crying. Liz breathes in and seems to work up her courage.

Mrs Beck, we are here to help you with some of the final decisions that need to be made. (*A beat.*) We need to be sure that you understand what we have just told you. We are here to answer any questions you might have . . . Do you understand that your husband is legally dead?

Cristina hangs her head in disbelief.

I know this may seem inappropriate, but there is a decision that needs to be made. We have a patient who is gravely ill. (*A beat.*) I'm here to give you some information about organ donation. Are you willing for your husband to donate his heart?

CLAUDIA
(*interrupting angrily*)
Can't we discuss this some other time?

LIZ
I'm afraid not. We'll give you time to discuss it, but it is a decision that has to be made quickly; his organs will not be suitable for ever

Cristina pulls away from her father and looks at the woman furiously.

CRISTINA
What the fuck are you talking about? My husband is still breathing and you want me to let you cut him open?

CLAUDIA

Can you leave us alone?

LIZ

Of course. Please take your time and consider it.

Cristina hides her head in her father's chest and he lets the doctor know with a look that he will convince her.

61. INT. PAUL'S ROOM — NIGHT

Paul and Mary sleep. Suddenly a sharp, insistent noise is heard. She wakes up, alarmed, and turns on the light.

MARY

Paul, Paul . . . the beeper . . .

Paul opens his eyes, sleepy, without understanding what is going on. Mary searches for the beeper desperately. She picks up some books, ruffles some shirts. She finds it, presses some buttons and reads the screen.

Paul . . . Paul . . . it's the hospital . . .

She goes to the phone and dials a number. She waits for a moment.

Ma'am, I'm calling on behalf of Paul Rivers.

A moment passes. Mary looks very worried.

Yes, ma'am, I understand. Where do I have to take him? OK, yes, I understand.

She hangs up and turns to Paul.

Let's go; they've got a heart.

62. INT. HALLWAY, HOSPITAL — NIGHT

Two male nurses wheel Paul down the hallway on a gurney. Mary walks beside him, holding his hand.

They reach the operating room, open the swinging doors and stop for a moment for Mary to say goodbye.

MARY

Good luck, my love.

She leans over to kiss him. They part and she tries to smile.

The nurses wheel Paul in and the doors close behind them. Mary remains alone in the hallway. She turns around and leaves.

63. INT. WAITING ROOM HOSPITAL — NIGHT

She heads towards the waiting room. A few feet away from her, Cristina walks by, devastated, holding her father's arm with Claudia next to her.

Mary watches them walk past and goes to sit on the same couch where Cristina received the news.

64. INT. CAFETERIA SPORTS CLUB — AFTERNOON

Cristina is sitting at a table drinking orange juice. Paul (dressed as he was in Scene 56, when he saw her get out of the pool) walks over to her.

PAUL

Hello.

Cristina, lost in thought, turns to look at him.

CRISTINA
(*surly*)

Hello.

Paul points at her left shoulder.

PAUL

Does your shoulder hurt?

CRISTINA

Why?

PAUL

Your stroke is too wide. If you tuck your arm in as you pull it back – (*Mimics the motion.*) – you'll glide better.

CRISTINA
(*dryly*)

Thanks for the advice.

Paul points at a chair.

PAUL

May I sit down?

CRISTINA

I was just leaving.

A waitress walks over and puts a sandwich in front of her.

PAUL

Just while you finish it, OK?

CRISTINA

No. Maybe next time.

PAUL
(*disappointed*)

Alright . . . bye . . .

He turns to leave, but returns after only a few steps.

Did you know that eating alone can seriously damage your kidneys?

Cristina can't help smiling. Paul bows his head to excuse himself and leaves.

65. EXT. STREET – NIGHT

Michael walks with his daughters (dressed as they were in Scene 2). He grabs his cellphone and dials a number.

MICHAEL

Hey, honey, we're on our way home. If you need me to pick up anything on the way, give me a call on my cellphone.

Laura spots a white cat a few yards away.

LAURA

Daddy, Daddy . . . a kitty . . .

The two girls move close to it.

> MICHAEL
> (*without putting the cellphone down*)
> Don't touch it . . . Laura, leave it . . .

The cat scurries away and the girls turn to look at it.

> OK, honey, I'll see you at home.

He hangs up. Lucio blows the leaves off a lawn. Michael and his daughters cross paths with him.

> LUCIO
> Goodnight, Mr Beck.

> MICHAEL
> Goodnight, Lucio. By the way, don't forget to do the garden on Saturday.

> LUCIO
> No sir, I won't forget.

Michael and his daughters continue on their way. Laura keeps looking at Lucio, who smiles at her.

66. INT. HALLWAY HOSPITAL – NIGHT

A door opens. Paul walks out. He is dressed in a hospital gown, dragging a rolling tripod from which hangs the IV connected to his arm.

He crosses the empty, silent hallway.

67. INT. NURSING STATION – CONTINUOUS

He arrives at an empty nursing station. He looks both ways. No one. He walks into the station and opens a filing cabinet. He checks it. He doesn't seem to find anything. He closes it and opens another drawer. As he is checking, he hears a woman's voice behind him.

> DOLORES
> (*out of shot*)
> Those are the records for children born at the hospital in March.

Paul turns around and bumps into Dolores, the nurse.

And in the other drawer are the records for children born in August.

Paul remains motionless on realising he's been caught.

You want some advice?

Pause.

Don't look any more. Trust me, you'll save yourself a lot of trouble.

PAUL
And what if I'm looking for trouble?

DOLORES
Whoever looks for the truth deserves the punishment for finding it and you can be sure you won't get it from this hospital. (*A beat.*) Now go to bed; you need the rest.

Paul walks out of the nursing station, slightly ashamed.

68. INT. CRISTINA'S ROOM — NIGHT

Cristina is alone in her room, drinking. A bottle of vodka and a carton of orange juice are on the bureau. Cristina looks sad and drunk. She grabs the phone and dials a number.

CRISTINA
Hello, is Ana there?

MALE VOICE
(*out of shot*)
Hang on a sec . . .

69. INTERCUT INT. BAR — CONTINUOUS

In a hip bar, the barman (who answered the telephone) calls out to a woman.

BARMAN
Ana, Ana . . . phone call . . .

Ana (thirty-six) answers the phone. She is an athletic, well-built woman packed into a lycra outfit, who looks like she has been around.

                          ANA
    Hello . . . hello . . .

70. INTERCUT INT. CRISTINA'S ROOM — CONTINUOUS

Cristina hears Ana pick up the phone and, nervous, hangs up.

71. INT. LIVING ROOM, JACK'S HOUSE — NIGHT

The living room looks empty and filthy, with bottles and plastic cups strewn all over. Trish picks up the mess.

We can hear noises. Trish goes to look out of the window and sees John and Marianne arrive in the old Pontiac.

72. EXT. JACK'S HOUSE — NIGHT

Marianne gets out of the car. Trish runs up to her.

                          TRISH
    What happened?

Marianne turns around to look at her, slightly dazed.

                        MARIANNE
    Did you get the people out?

                          TRISH
    Yeah. I told them your dad got sick and you and Jack went to see him.

                        MARIANNE
    Where's Jack?

                          TRISH
    In the kids' room.

Marianne walks towards the house.

73. INT. CHILDREN'S ROOM, JACK'S HOUSE — NIGHT

She opens the door, taking care to not make noise. The room is dimly lit. Jack is sitting between his children's beds, watching them, taciturn.

Marianne stands in front of him. Feeling her presence, Jack lifts his face and looks her in the eye.

> JACK
>
> Did you go?

She nods, then bends down and kneels.

> Are they dead?

Marianne nods again. Jack has a pained expression on his face. He looks at Gina, who sleeps peacefully.

> I'm turning myself in tomorrow.

> MARIANNE
>
> John says nobody saw you, nobody. They don't know the licence plates or what car it was. Some asshole even swears it was a cab.

Jack lifts Marianne off her knees and stands up.

> JACK
>
> What would you do if these were our children? Tell me: what?

Marianne stands up and faces him.

> MARIANNE
>
> They're not; it didn't happen to us.

> JACK
> *(raising his voice)*
>
> No, it didn't happen to us; it happened to me, understand: me. I saw those girls dying and I ran away . . .

The children stir in their beds from the voices. Jack leaves the room.

74. INT. LIVING ROOM, JACK'S HOUSE — CONTINUOUS

He walks through the living room past John and Trish's awestruck stare and into his room, followed by Marianne.

49

75. INT. ROOM, JACK'S HOUSE — CONTINUOUS

> MARIANNE
>
> What the fuck do you gain by turning yourself in?

> JACK
>
> It's my duty.

> MARIANNE
>
> Your duty is here with us, with your family.

> JACK
>
> My duty is to God.

Jack dodges her, walks into the bathroom and locks the door.

> MARIANNE
>
> Jack, please.

She leans on the door, distressed.

76. INT. KITCHEN, CRISTINA'S HOUSE — EVENING

We see Cristina standing in front of the oven. She puts a cake in and adjusts the temperature. She looks happy, relaxed.

> KATIE
> (*out of shot*)
>
> Do I put the chocolate chips in now, Mommy?

Sitting at the kitchen table, Laura and Katie (dressed as they were in Scene 2) are making another cake. The table is covered with spilt flour, eggshells. Laura whisks some eggs in a bowl.

> CRISTINA
>
> Yes, sweetie, and then stir.

Katie empties a cup of chocolate chips into a larger bowl and then starts mixing them in with a wooden spoon. Laura stops whisking.

> LAURA
>
> Mommy, I'm tired.

> CRISTINA
>
> Here, I'll give you a hand.

Cristina sits down and the girl sits in her lap. Between them they take the whisk and start mixing.

LAURA
What time is Daddy coming?

CRISTINA
He'll pick you up any second now.

Cristina stirs with Laura while Katie decorates the cake.

77. INT. DINING ROOM, PAUL'S APARTMENT — DAY

A heart-shaped cake is at the centre of the table. The frosting is decorated with 'Welcome Home' in red icing.

A cake knife cuts out a slice. The camera pulls back and we see Paul sitting at the head of the table and Mary cutting the cake. Several friends surround them and some kids run around.

Mary serves Paul a large slice. He forks a piece into his mouth.

FRIEND 1
Didn't the doctors say you're not supposed to pig out?

PAUL
(*spraying cake crumbs*)
I've got to make up for lost time.

FRIEND 2
Lost time, not lost pounds. We're going to have to take you back for liposuction.

The guests laugh. Paul raises a glass of water.

PAUL
Here's to those who believed I wasn't going to die.

EVERYONE
Here, here.

Paul hugs Mary.

PAUL
Cheers, on the first day of my new life.

51

Cheers.

They raise their glasses and drink. Once they have finished, Mary taps her glass with a knife.

MARY

I also have an announcement to make.

The rest of the guests grow quiet. A mother holds on to one of her children to prevent him from running around.

MARIA

I want to tell you that Paul and I are going to be parents.

Paul looks at her, stupefied; the others, surprised. A friend quickly congratulates her.

FEMALE FRIEND I

You kept this real quiet . . .

MARY

Well, we're going to be parents, but we don't know when yet. I'm going to have an operation and then we're going to try artificial insemination . . .

MALE FRIEND I

Artificial insemination? (*to Paul*) Can't cope with the natural ways any more? Don't let your female students find out . . .

He stretches out his finger and slowly lets it drop. His wife pulls his arm.

WIFE

Alan . . .

Paul forces a smile and turns to look at Mary, irritated.

78. INT. FUNERAL HOME — DAY

Cristina is surrounded by her father, Claudia, her parents-in-law, her aunts and friends.

In the middle of the chapel are three coffins: an adult coffin and two small, white ones for children.

> FATHER
>
> You want me to bring you something to eat?

> CRISTINA
>
> I'm not hungry.

> FATHER
>
> You need to eat something.

Cristina shakes her head. Her father grabs her by the hand.

> When your mother died, I thought I wasn't going to make it. I felt the world was falling on me and that I was never going to get up, but life goes on, sweetie . . .

Cristina looks at him harshly and lets go of his hand.

> CRISTINA
>
> You know what I thought when my mother died? I couldn't understand how you could laugh again, how you could talk to people again, how you could play with us. And no, Dad, that's a lie: life does not go on.

Upset, she stands up to go sit somewhere else.

79. INT. BOWLING ALLEY – DAY

A private investigator (fifty-five) – bald, with a spade beard – is standing before a bowling lane, ball in hand. He starts off, slides and lets the ball go. There are two pins at the end of the lane. He only knocks down one of them.

He turns around and smacks his left palm with his right fist.

> PRIVATE INVESTIGATOR
>
> Shit!

He goes to sit down. A group of his friends make fun of him, but he does not pay very much attention to them. He sees Paul arrive.

> PAUL
>
> Mr Donneaud?

The private investigator goes to greet him.

PRIVATE INVESTIGATOR

Mr Rivers, thank you for coming, but I couldn't cancel this appointment.

He points at his friends and bursts into laughter. He drinks his beer and leads him to a small table. They sit down.

Please, sit down. When did you say you had surgery?

PAUL

May the second. The man that gave me his heart must have died that day or the day before.

One of his friends rolls a strike and turns to him, boasting. He grabs his beer and toasts with him. He them turns to Paul.

PRIVATE INVESTIGATOR

It's hard work, pal. Hospitals don't give up that kind of information; they're scared shitless of lawsuits.

He sips his beer and wipes off his moustache. One of his friends calls him.

FRIEND

You're up.

PRIVATE INVESTIGATOR

Roll for me, I'll be there in a second. (*to Paul*) It's going to cost you five thousand plus expenses, but I guarantee results. I need two grand in advance.

PAUL

That's a bit expensive, isn't it?

PRIVATE INVESTIGATOR

I'll even find out what kind of underwear the guy wore.

PAUL

I don't have any money on me, but I can send a cheque to your office.

The private investigator smiles and signals around him.

PRIVATE INVESTIGATOR

The world is my office and this – (*Shows him a cellphone.*) – is my secretary. Can you give the cheque now?

Paul pulls out a pen and starts to fill in the cheque. The private investigator drinks from his beer.

Hey, what does it feel like to have somebody else's heart?

Paul thinks about the question.

PAUL
Better than some people with their own brain.

The private investigator is amused by the answer. He tips his beer towards Paul.

PRIVATE INVESTIGATOR
Cheers.

Paul answers the toast by bowing his head slightly.

80. EXT. JACK'S HOUSE — NIGHT

Marianne is in front of the bloodstained Ford Lobo. Below her is a bucket full of water.

She takes out a wet rag and starts scrubbing the blood forcefully. She cleans and cleans until she collapses, exhausted, on the hood of the truck.

81. INT. DINING ROOM PAUL'S APARTMENT — AFTERNOON

Remnants of cake and dirty plates lie on the dining-room table. Mary, dressed as she was in Scene 77, at Paul's welcome party, cleans up while Paul watches her, sitting in a chair.

MARY
Louise is getting fat, don't you think?

Paul doesn't answer. He just looks at her picking up plates.

She's done nothing but eat since Robert left her.

Mary stacks up the dishes, turns and sees Paul staring at her.

What? She looks OK to you?

PAUL
Why did you tell everybody about us having kids?

55

Mary is surprised by the question.

> MARY
>
> I wanted to share our plans with them.

Paul stands up and walks towards her.

> PAUL
>
> You said it: 'our plans'. People have no reason to know about our private life.

> MARY
>
> Why the fuss? They're our best friends.

> PAUL
>
> We haven't even talked about it.

Mary stops cleaning.

> MARY
>
> Oh, we haven't? I thought this was more than settled.

> PAUL
>
> Things changed, Mary. We have to think this over.

> MARY
>
> I don't have anything to think over; I've already made my decision. (*Points at some glasses.*) Would you help me with the glasses?

She lifts the stack of plates and takes them into the kitchen. Paul watches her walk in and then starts picking up the glasses.

82. INT. LIVING ROOM CRISTINA'S HOUSE — AFTERNOON

In the living room are Cristina, Claudia, her father and several other family members. You can almost breathe the silence. Everyone talks in whispers. Cristina is sunk in a sofa, dressed in black.

Claudia gets up with her glass and heads towards the kitchen. Cristina follows her.

83. INT. KITCHEN CRISTINA'S HOUSE — AFTERNOON

Cristina walks into the kitchen. She grabs a bottle of tequila from a table with sodas, brandy and ice. She serves herself some in her glass and drinks.

Claudia walks in and stares at her.

> CLAUDIA
>
> Take it easy.

Cristina, challenging, knocks back the entire contents of the glass and serves herself some more before Claudia's disapproving stare.

> CRISTINA
>
> I know what I'm doing.

Claudia takes two steps towards her and looks her in the eyes.

> CLAUDIA
>
> Cris, they called and said that the culprit turned himself in today. He called the police himself. His name is Jack Jordan. (*Pause.*) They said you need to go press charges. I'll go with you if you want.

Cristina turns to look at her absently.

> CRISTINA
>
> I'm not going to do anything.

> CLAUDIA
>
> The guy was some ex-con who's spent half his life in jail. Are you going to let someone like him walk the streets?

> CRISTINA
>
> What do you want me to do?

> CLAUDIA
> (*pained*)
>
> He ran over Michael, your daughters . . .

> CRISTINA
>
> Stay out of this.

Cristina drinks.

CLAUDIA

Stay out of this? They were my family too, my nieces, I had
to identify the bodies, I was the one who saw them dead.
You have to do something.

CRISTINA

What for? Nothing I can do is going to bring them back.

*She looks downcast, in despair. She looks at her sister and drinks down
all the tequila in her glass again.*

84. INT. RESTAURANT — DAY

*It is a pretentious restaurant decorated in bad taste, where some
middle-class families eat. The private investigator is sitting at a table.*

*Paul finds him just as he is about to bite into a sandwich. He stands
up on seeing Paul and invites him to sit down.*

PRIVATE INVESTIGATOR

How're you doing?

PAUL

Well.

PRIVATE INVESTIGATOR

Want some?

*He shows him the sandwich and Paul shakes his head. The private
investigator grabs his briefcase and takes out a folder.*

The man who gave you your heart was called Michael
Beck. He was thirty-seven years old, an architect and
married.

He takes out some photocopies from the folder.

This is the transplant authorisation signed by his wife,
Cristina Williams, and this is a copy of the medical report.
Here's the widow's phone number and address in case
you're interested.

He spreads out the papers and Paul looks over them.

What did Michael Beck die of?

It was a real tragedy. Some guy called Jack Jordan ran over
him and his two little girls on May the second at seven
twenty p.m.

*He shows Paul a newspaper cut-out. The headline reads: 'Madman
Runs over Family'. Underneath is the photograph of one of the girls'
bodies covered by a white sheet.*

This Jordan guy's really something. He's been in and out
of the joint since he was sixteen. The last time they locked
him up was 'cause he let off a shot while he was mugging
someone and he hit a pregnant woman walking by. God
knows how the woman survived, but he went fucking nuts
with guilt and punched his cell walls until he cracked his
wrists and hands. He got out just two years ago.

*Paul takes the cut-out and looks at it. He pales and starts breathing
with difficulty. The private investigator is frightened at seeing him like
this.*

Are you alright?

*Paul brings his hand to his heart, pressing it as if he were trying to
calm something inside him.*

Do you want some water?

Paul lifts his hand up to signal he is better.

85. EXT. BASKETBALL COURT SCHOOL – DAY

*Several boys and girls about Katie and Laura's age are standing in
line. Their expressions are serious and pained.*

*Some mothers are in the back of the court. In the middle are Claudia
and Cristina, both dressed in black, with sunglasses.*

A picture of Katie and one of Laura sit on a desk at the front.

*A priest (fifty) – grey hair, glasses, dressed in a dark suit – addresses
the group.*

Katie and Laura have gone and it is hard for us to explain why. Why did two sweet girls have to leave so soon? We get angry at God, and with good reason. I am also angry at him because he snatched them away from us like this. But we must trust that now they are by his side, that God called them to fill their hearts with the infinite love that only he can give . . .

Claudia cries quietly. So do some of the mothers. Cristina remains imperturbable.

86. EXT. PATIO – DAY

Claudia and Cristina are in the middle of a patio. Some mothers walk over to offer their condolences.

MOTHER 1

I'm very sorry, Cristina.

She hugs her. Another woman walks over and also hugs her.

MOTHER 2

If you need anything, count on me.

The children return to their classrooms. Cristina whispers in Claudia's ear.

CRISTINA

I'll be right back.

87. INT. BATHROOM SCHOOL – MOMENTS LATER

Cristina is standing in front of the mirror. She takes her dark glasses off and looks at herself for a while. She opens her purse, takes out a small bag of cocaine, spoons some out with the top of a ballpoint pen and snorts it.

She looks at herself in the mirror again. Behind her is a five-year-old girl, watching her silently.

Cristina turns to look at her. They stare at each other for a few seconds without saying anything.

A teacher wearing an apron pokes her head through the door.

> TEACHER
> (*to the girl*)
> Hurry up, Tracy, classes have already started.

The girl grabs her teacher's hand and walks out without taking her eyes off Cristina.

88. INT. KITCHEN PAUL'S APARTMENT — NIGHT

Paul walks into the kitchen and turns on the light. He walks towards the refrigerator, pulls out a carton of milk and pours some into a glass.

Mary walks in and leans on the wall.

> MARY
> You could come in and say hello.

Paul turns to look at her.

> PAUL
> Sorry, I thought you were asleep.

He walks over and kisses her on the cheek. She receives it coldly.

> MARY
> It's eleven o'clock at night, Paul. They've been calling you from the university all day long. May I ask what you did today?

> PAUL
> Stuff, drive around . . .

> MARY
> You had me worried. The doctor told you to take it easy. I didn't know if something had happened.

> PAUL
> I'm fine, nothing happened.

He takes a sip of his milk and pulls out, from his pocket, a newspaper cut-out, folded in four. He spreads it out on the washbasin.

> I know whose heart it was. He was an architect . . .

Mary shakes her head in disapproval.

> MARY
>
> Why did you find out? What for?

> PAUL
>
> He left a widow . . .

> MARY
>
> What's the point in getting involved?

> PAUL
>
> I need to know who I am now.

> MARY
>
> I don't think that's the way to do it.

> PAUL
>
> Then which is?

> MARY
>
> Look for it with me. Let's look ahead together, not behind.

They remain silent for a long while.

> Don't forget that we have an appointment with the
> gynaecologist tomorrow at eleven . . .

She turns around and walks away. Paul watches her leave, drinking his milk.

89. EXT. BAR – DUSK

Jack and Brown leave the bar. They stand on the sidewalk. Brown looks slightly drunk; Jack doesn't.

> BROWN
>
> Dammit Jack, it's your birthday and you didn't even have
> one drink with me. You should never trust someone who
> doesn't drink.

> JACK
>
> And you should never trust pussies who talk such
> Barbie-doll bullshit.

Pause.

Why don't you come to my place? I'm having a party.

BROWN

Yeah, great party, I bet they're all as boring as you are.

JACK

You'd be surprised . . .

BROWN

Nah, I'll pass.

Jack sees the wristwatch on Brown's arm and turns it towards him to see the time.

JACK

Shit, it's late, I've got to go. See ya . . .

BROWN

I'll call you later about the job. OK?

JACK

Hey, Brown, you should.

BROWN

Yeah, I will.

They say goodbye by knocking fists. Jack walks quickly towards his truck.

90. EXT. DESERT – DAY

Paul quickly walks down a trail mechanically. He is carrying a revolver in his hand (the same one from Scene 12 where he talks to Cristina by the empty pool).

He stops at the edge of the road, tucks the revolver away in his waist and leans on a mesquite. He is pale and shaking.

He breathes in and goes on his way with difficulty.

91. INT. DOCTOR'S OFFICE – DAY

Mary and Paul are sitting before the gynaecologist. Paul looks completely recovered.

GYNAECOLOGIST
(*to Mary*)
Could you have the surgery on Monday?

Mary turns to look at Paul, who nods.

MARY
Yes.

PAUL
What percentage chance does Mary have of getting
pregnant?

GYNAECOLOGIST
I can't offer you a real number. There was some damage
from the previous abortion. It wasn't treated properly and
that . . .

PAUL
What abortion?

*Paul lets go of Mary's hand and turns to look at her, distressed. Mary
fires a look at the doctor.*

92. INT. OFFICE HALLWAY — DAY

*Paul is standing next to the elevators, furious. He presses the 'down'
button. Mary is standing behind him.*

MARY
I can explain.

PAUL
Explain what?

MARY
There – is – an – explanation . . .

PAUL
(*facing her*)
Why did you kick up such a fuss about artificial insemination,
the pictures of our friends' babies everywhere, the toys, the
kids' room, the kids' names? Why? To flush them down the

64

toilet? (*A beat.*) It's been a long time since we've had anything to do with each other.

MARY

Oh yeah? Why didn't you tell me that when you were sick? Huh? Or did you expect one of your girlfriends to come and take care of you?

PAUL

You came back because you wanted to. Don't blame it on me now.

MARY

I came back to take care of you because I love you.

PAUL

Or was it because you were feeling lonely?

This seems seriously to humiliate Mary. Tears well up in her and she drops her eyes.

I'm sorry.

An empty elevator opens but Paul does not walk in. The doors close and they stand there.

Mary, our relationship couldn't go any further. This whole thing about the child, the insemination, they're just patches for something that's already finished.

MARY

It isn't finished if we give it a chance and have this baby.

Paul looks her in the eyes.

PAUL

When we could have, you didn't want it. Let it go.

MARY

We were separated, goddammit! It's different now.

PAUL

Yes, it is different. Precisely.

A couple walk out of a doctor's office, pass behind them, watch them argue and get into the elevator.

MARY

You only know how to think about yourself.

PAUL

Yes. Now more than ever.

An elevator opens. Mary walks in and he stays outside.

93. INT. HALLWAY CRISTINA'S HOUSE — AFTERNOON

Cristina is standing in front of the door to her daughters' room (same as Scene 41). She is about to go in but cannot. She stands there holding on to the handle.

She cannot open the door. She leans on it and breathes deeply for a few seconds. She swallows and walks away.

94. INT. PRISON HALLWAY — DAY

John walks down the hallway escorted by two guards. A prisoner walks up to him and bows slightly. John grabs the prisoner by the shoulders.

JOHN

We haven't spoken in a while. See you tomorrow at eleven?

PRISONER

Yes, Reverend.

John keeps walking until he reaches Jack's cell. John walks in and finds him lying on his bed, motionless, with his eyes open, staring at the roof.

95. INT. JACK'S CELL — DAY

On hearing him walk in, Jack turns to look at John. He gets up weakly and sits on the cot.

JOHN

How are you?

Jack doesn't answer. John sits down next to him.

They tell me you don't want to eat . . .

Jack fixes his eyes on the floor.

> Jack, Jesus didn't come to free us from pain. He came to give us the strength to bear it.

JACK
Jesus wanted this pain for me.

JOHN
He had nothing to do with this, it was an accident.

Jack lifts his head and looks John in the eyes.

JACK
No, this wasn't an accident. Jesus chose me for this . . .

John stands up and leans against the wall.

JOHN
Ask for the mercy of Jesus Christ.

JACK
If it was an accident, why do I have to ask for his mercy?
(*A beat.*) 'I will have mercy on whom I will have mercy, and I will have compassion on whom I will have compassion.'
Romans, 9:15.

JOHN
Don't be so prideful, that's a sin . . .

Jack starts to orate uncontrollably.

JACK
'The fearful, and unbelieving, and the abominable, and murderers, and whoremongers, and sorcerers, and . . .

JOHN
Listen to me, Jack, listen to me . . .

JACK
. . . idolaters, and all liars . . .

JOHN
Jesus came to save us, not to damn us . . .

. . . shall have their part in the lake which burneth with fire and brimstone.' Revelation, 21:8.

John points to Jack's 'Jesus loves you' tattoo on his forearm.

JOHN

Jesus loves you, but he also knows how to punish arrogant sinners like you.

JACK

'As many as I love I rebuke and chasten . . .' Revelation, 3:19

They are silent for a few moments.

Jesus betrayed me . . .

JOHN

Stop your stupid shit or you're going straight to hell.

JACK

This is hell, right here . . .

JOHN

You're damning your soul; shut up now and ask Jesus Christ to forgive you.

JACK

Forgive me? I did everything he asked me to do. I changed, I gave him my life and he betrayed me . . .

John looks gravely offended. His eyes light up and he can barely contain his rage. But Jack keeps staring at John with even more fiery eyes.

He put that truck in my hands to carry out his fucking will. He made me kill those girls and didn't give me the strength to stay and save them.

John faces him, angry, losing control.

JOHN

Don't blaspheme, you bastard. Christ had nothing to do with this . . .

JACK

God even knows when a single hair moves on your head . . .
(*Jack points his index finger at John.*) And you taught me
that.

*John is speechless. Jack sits back down on his bed and pays no further
attention to John.*

96. EXT. BAR STREET — NIGHT

*Cristina's car stops in front of a bar. A valet walks up to her, opens her
door and hands her a ticket. She heads for the bar.*

*Paul's car also pulls up in front of the bar. He gets out and another
valet hands him a ticket.*

97. INT. BAR — NIGHT

*It is the same bar from Scene 69. It is crowded with twenty-seven,
twenty-eight-year-olds. Cristina dodges her way around them, makes
her way to the bar and calls the bartender.*

CRISTINA

Absolut, straight up, please.

*The bartender pours her a shot. She knocks it down and gestures for
him to serve her some more. The bartender obliges and fills the glass up.*

Do you know where Ana is?

The bartender points at some tables at the back of the room.

BARTENDER

She's over there.

98. POINT OF VIEW BAR — CONTINUOUS

*From the back of the bar, Paul watches Cristina walk towards a table
where Ana is sitting with some other people. On noticing her arrival,
Ana stands up and hugs Cristina enthusiastically. They talk about
something Paul cannot hear.*

Ana grabs Cristina by the arm and impels her to follow her.

Ana and Cristina walk in. A young woman is checking her make-up in front of the mirror. Ana stares at her defiantly. The young woman hurries up and leaves.

Ana bolts the door and turns around to look at Cristina.

> ANA
>
> Cristi, Cristi, Cristi, I can't believe it. Just like old times, huh?

Cristina nods with an emotionless smile. Ana lifts herself up to sit beside the sink and puts her bag next to her.

> What happened to you? Did you finally end up marrying that hunk you brought that time?

> CRISTINA
>
> Yes.

> ANA
>
> And so, was he a good lay?

Cristina doesn't answer and just swallows. Ana looks at her cheerfully.

> Oh men, men . . . How they make us suffer . . .

She smiles and opens her bag.

> You came just at the right time; I've got all sorts of candy.

She pulls out an assortment of drugs from her bag and lines them up on the counter. Someone knocks on the door.

> It's busy.

They stop knocking and Ana points at each bag.

> Angel dust, Special K, the old-time favourite cocaine and the newest of the new: R-2.

She pulls out a tiny ziploc bag with several pills and gets off the sink.

> They're all the rage: two of these will send you straight to heaven.

Cristina looks at the pills sceptically.

CRISTINA

I'm not into chemicals.

ANA

Cristi, you're not like that. Are you a cuddly kitty now?
Take two now, on the house, and if you don't like 'em,
don't buy 'em. OK?

*Cristina takes two, looks at Ana and grabs another two. She swallows
all four down with tap water. Ana raises her eyebrows.*

That's my girl. Just take it easy on the booze, OK? We don't
want you stuck in the other side of heaven.

*Cristina looks at her deprecatively. She grabs the bag of coke, a fistful
of pills and puts them in her purse.*

100. INT. BATHROOMS JAIL — NIGHT

*The bathrooms are decorated with chipped green and white tiles. There
is a row of open showers. A fat prisoner with an eagle tattooed on his
back bathes in a cloud of steam.*

*Jack sits barefoot on a bench in front of the showers. He wears a white
sleeveless T-shirt and prison-uniform pants. Taciturn, he stares at the
water running into the drain.*

*The prisoner finishes and starts to dry himself. He looks at Jack, who
is still motionless.*

PRISONER

Hurry up: there's roll-call at eight.

*Jack doesn't pay attention. The prisoner covers himself up with the
towel and walks towards the dressing rooms. Jack watches him leave.
He stands up and pulls the bench towards the showers.*

*He stands on the bench, ties one of his shirtsleeves to the shower head
and the other to his neck. He sighs, kicks the bench away and hangs.*

*His body is starting to go limp when the shower head suddenly breaks.
Jack falls on his ass.*

Upon hearing the noise, the other prisoner runs into the bathroom.

He finds Jack sprawled out on the tiles, getting soaked by the water flowing out of the broken shower head, with his shirtsleeves tied around his neck.

When he sees the fat prisoner looking at him worriedly, Jack starts laughing to himself.

101. EXT. BAR — NIGHT

Cristina exits the bar with a drink in her hand. She looks very high and very drunk. She stumbles over to the valets and gives one of them her ticket.

She stands on the sidewalk, waiting for her car. Paul walks out and watches her from a few yards away.

A valet arrives with the car and opens the door. She is about to get in when the valet holds her by the arm and points at her drink.

> VALET
> Ma'am, you can't take that glass . . .

> CRISTINA
> Get out of my way . . .

> VALET
> You're in no condition to drive.

> CRISTINA
> What the fuck do you care, asshole?

Cristina pushes him, gets in and slams the door shut. She steps on the accelerator and drives. The valet moves out of the way to avoid being run over.

Cristina's car goes twenty yards before it rides up on the sidewalk. The valets and Paul run towards her.

They find her leaning on the wheel, muttering curses. A valet puts his hand through the open window and opens the door. Cristina turns to him, furious.

> Get away from me, you fuck . . .

She throws a punch that the valet manages to dodge. Paul gets in the way.

> PAUL
> (*to the valet*)
> Excuse me ... (*to Cristina*) Cristina, I can drive you home ...

Cristina looks at him with glassy eyes.

> CRISTINA
> Who the hell are you?

> PAUL
> Your friend from the sports club.

Several valets surround the car.

> CRISTINA
> Tell these motherfuckers to go away.

Paul asks them to leave with a gesture from his hand. Slowly, the valets move away.

> PAUL
> You can't drive like this.

> CRISTINA
> What do you care?

A patrol car crosses the next block and he points at it.

> PAUL
> You're going to get arrested. Let me drive ... please.

Cristina sees the patrol car pass and sighs. She looks around her: there are curious onlookers and valets scrutinising her. She is too high and drunk to protest, and docilely slides over to the co-pilot seat.

102. INT. CRISTINA'S CAR — MOMENTS LATER

Paul drives. She sleeps soundly beside him.

They arrive at Cristina's house. Paul searches the visor for the garage door remote. He presses it and the door opens. He parks the car.

103. INT. CAR/GARAGE — CONTINUOUS

Paul shuts off the engine. Cristina does not wake up. Paul pushes the co-pilot seat back and leaves her half-lying down. He takes off his olive-green jacket, bundles it up and puts it under her head as a pillow.

He looks at her for a few seconds and softly caresses her forehead. He then takes the keys out of the ignition and hides them under the rug. He presses the garage-door remote.

104. EXT. GARAGE — CONTINUOUS

The electric door starts closing. Paul runs out.

105. INT. VISITING ROOM JAIL — DAY

Marianne sits in a room with a table and three chairs, lit by a dusty, bare, sixty-watt bulb. It is dark, cold and windowless.

Jack walks in escorted by two guards and sits down in front of her. The guards retire to the door.

> MARIANNE
>
> How are you doing?

Jack shrugs his shoulders.

> JACK
>
> How are the kids?

> MARIANNE
>
> They won't stop asking about you. (*A beat.*) I told them you went on a trip.

> JACK
>
> Why didn't you tell them the truth?

> MARIANNE
>
> What for?

> JACK
>
> Lying is a sin, Marianne.

They are quiet for a few seconds. Marianne, nervous, wets her lips before she goes on.

MARIANNE

I sold the truck to pay for the lawyer. You'll be out on probation real soon.

JACK

I didn't ask for a lawyer.

Marianne exhales, exasperated. She opens her purse, takes out her children's grade reports and puts them on the table.

MARIANNE

The kids' grades. Gina did good, but Freddy had four detentions for misconduct. He'd gotten very good grades and now he's doing terribly. (*A beat.*) The kids need you. I need you . . .

JACK

I can't leave here . . .

MARIANNE

Do you want your children to spend another five years without you? Is that what you want?

JACK

This is God's will . . .

MARIANNE

Four years ago you didn't believe in anything, and now everything has to do with God.

Jack fixes his eyes on her. She is not intimidated.

I preferred you the way you were before.

JACK

Before? I was a fucking beast, before. Is that who you prefer?

MARIANNE

At least that was you. Now I don't have the slightest fucking idea who you are.

Marianne gets up and heads towards the door. Before she leaves she turns around.

Life has to go on, Jack, with or without God . . .

She crosses between the two door guards. Jack rests his elbow on the table and rubs his head.

106. EXT. HALLWAY HIGHWAY MOTEL — DAY/DAWN

Cristina, dressed in shorts and a black T-shirt, is leaning on the hallway banister. In the distance, we can see the lights from the cars driving down the highway. The sun is about to rise.

She takes long drinks from a bottle of tequila. She pulls out a plastic bag, opens it: there are several R-2 pills. She takes four and washes them down with a drink. She turns around to go into the room.

107. INT. BATHROOM HIGHWAY MOTEL — CONTINUOUS

Cristina sits on the bed. She sees Paul asleep and strokes his forehead tenderly. She takes one last swill from the bottle of tequila. She leaves it on the nightstand, almost empty, lies down and closes her eyes.

108. EXT. STREET — DAY

A '93 Malibu is parked on a street in a working-class neighbourhood. Paul arrives in his car and parks behind it.

He steps out of the car, and gets into the Malibu.

109. INT. MALIBU — DAY

Inside the Malibu is the private investigator.

> PRIVATE INVESTIGATOR
> Hey.

> PAUL
> Hey. Did you get what I asked for?

The private investigator rummages in his jacket pocket and takes out a paper folded in two.

> PRIVATE INVESTIGATOR
> Jordan lives in a cheap motel lost in the middle of nowhere. It looks like one of his prison-fishy pals is from there. The motel's address and phone number is on there.

PAUL

That was quick.

PRIVATE INVESTIGATOR

Piece of cake, friend. Just a matter of checking the calls.

He shows him a phone bill where a phone number is highlighted in yellow. He takes out some photographs of Jack's police record and shows them to him.

These are recent photos of Jordan from his last stay in jail.

Paul looks at them and puts them away.

PAUL

And what about the other thing?

The private investigator looks at both sides of the street. He opens the glove compartment and pulls out a red terrycloth that is wrapped around something.

He puts it on the seat and spreads it out. Inside is a .38 Smith and Wesson (the same from Scene 12, where Paul shows Cristina the empty shells) and eight golden bullets.

PRIVATE INVESTIGATOR

Clean gun, no record.

Paul tries to open the cylinder but cannot. The private investigator gestures for Paul to give him the gun. He skilfully opens the cylinder and puts the bullets in.

He closes the cylinder and leaves the gun loaded.

To shoot, you just have to cock it.

He shows him how to do it, then puts the hammer back in place and hands Paul the loaded gun.

There you go. Is it to kill this guy?

PAUL

No, just in case.

PRIVATE INVESTIGATOR

If you kill him, don't say I sold it to you.

Paul pulls out an envelope and hands it to the private investigator. He opens it, counts the money and puts it in his jacket pocket.

We're set then.

Paul hides the gun in his clothes and gets out of the car.

110. REHAB CENTER — DAY

Cristina is in a rehabilitation session. The group listens to a skinny, unpleasant woman (forty-eight), who speaks excitedly, on the verge of crying.

> SKINNY WOMAN
> They were terrible months. My husband didn't even touch me. And I felt lonely and ugly and I was only happy when I was at parties where I could drink and make jokes and have fun . . .

Cristina listens to her, annoyed. She looks uncomfortable.

> And I didn't care if my husband got angry, because he had his things and I had mine and then I met . . .

Cristina stares absently to her right and left and suddenly stands up. She walks towards the door and leaves.

111. INT. LIVING ROOM JACK'S HOUSE — DAY

Marianne walks through the living room with the hamster cage. Following her in a tantrum is Freddy, with Gina who looks ill, sniffling and teary.

> FREDDY
> Mommy, don't give him away . . .

> MARIANNE
> The hair is making your sister sick, can't you see?

> FREDDY
> Yeah, but don't give him away.

> GINA
> Yeah, Mom, don't give him away.

Marianne turns to look at Gina in disbelief. She walks towards the back door that leads to the patio, opens it and leaves. Her children follow her closely.

112. EXT. BACK PATIO JACK'S HOUSE — CONTINUOUS

Marianne takes the hamster outside.

> FREDDY
> We can shave him so he doesn't have hair.

Marianne turns to look at him, with the trace of a smile.

> MARIANNE
> Honey, no . . . Look . . . I'm going to buy you each a frog . . . OK?

> GINA
> I'm scared of frogs . . .

> MARIANNE
> Alright, a turtle . . .

Freddy is still upset.

> FREDDY
> You don't want the hamster because Daddy gave it to us and you don't love Daddy any more.

Marianne, worried, turns to Freddy.

> MARIANNE
> That's stupid.

She throws the hamster cage and goes inside. Her children, awestruck, run after her.

113. INT. VESTIBULE SPORTS CLUB — EVENING

It is raining torrentially in the street. Cristina – wearing sweatpants, tennis shoes and carrying a gym bag – is standing near the main entrance. She peers out every few moments into the street and only sees total gridlock.

She takes out her cellphone and dials a number.

CRISTINA

Ma'am, it's been an hour since I called for a taxi . . . yes . . .
46 St Vincent Street, please.

She hangs up, annoyed.

PAUL
(*out of shot*)

Hello.

*Cristina turns around and sees Paul, who, smoking, smiles at her
confidently, as if they knew each other. Cristina stares as if she were
trying to recognise him.*

CRISTINA

Hello.

Paul points at the leaden sky.

PAUL

I don't think it's going to stop raining. (*A beat.*) Do you
have a car?

CRISTINA

No, but my taxi'll be here in a minute.

*What she says seems absurd. No cars are moving in the insane
gridlock and tremendous downpour.*

PAUL

I can give you a ride if you want.

*Cristina looks at him, hesitant. She peers out at the street with the
hope that her taxi will arrive. She only sees cars moving
exasperatingly slowly.*

CRISTINA

No thanks.

She looks out again. Paul stands next to her.

PAUL

I was the one who drove your car home last week.

Cristina is slightly stunned. She stares at him as if she were almost able to recognise him.

CRISTINA
(*slightly embarrassed*)
I'm sorry, I don't remember.

PAUL
I left you my jacket . . .

Cristina and Paul stare at each other until she lowers her gaze.

CRISTINA
I'm really sorry. I'll bring it tomorrow.

PAUL
Really, I can give you a ride.

CRISTINA
No thanks, my cab won't be long.

She looks out again. Suddenly Paul starts speaking.

PAUL
I was an Eagle Scout, I was on the honour roll in secondary school and I won second place in a music contest in high school. I bought my first *Playboy* when I was fifteen. I've smoked twenty joints, I've been in nine street fights and only lost two. I used to believe in Santa Claus when I was a boy. I don't believe in him any more but I still secretly hope that one day he'll bring me presents again. My name is Paul Rivers, I'm a forty-one-year-old university professor of advanced maths with a guilty fascination for Britney Spears. I know that when you were a little girl they told you not to speak to strangers, but now you know things about me that most people don't. Therefore, I'm not a stranger any more. So, do you want a ride home?

Cristina is half-amused and half-dazed at Paul's sudden speech. He looks at her, waiting for an answer.

114. INT. CAR — EVENING

They get into the car, soaked. Cristina shakes some water off her hair and puts her bag on the floor of the back seat. She looks at the ashtray: it is full of cigarette butts. She opens the window.

Paul holds out his hand.

> PAUL
> Let me introduce myself again: I'm Paul Rivers.

Cristina shakes his hand.

> CRISTINA
> Cristina Beck.

> PAUL
> It's a pleasure to meet you, Cristina Beck.

Paul starts the car. Cristina begins to relax.

115. EXT. HIGHWAY MOTEL — EVENING

The truck that transports the processing-plant workers pulls over next to the motel. Jack hurdles over the back and lands on the ground. He knocks twice and the truck leaves.

Tired and dirty, Jack watches the truck leave and heads for the motel.

116. EXT. HALLWAY, HIGHWAY MOTEL — CONTINUOUS

Jack walks down the motel hallway. Suddenly a door opens and Paul walks out of a room. They meet face to face. Their eyes cross and Paul becomes uneasy.

> JACK
> 'Evening.

Jack continues on his way and Paul watches him until he walks into his room five doors down.

117. EXT. CRISTINA'S HOUSE — EVENING

Paul parks the car in front of Cristina's house. It is still slightly drizzling. Nightfall is imminent.

> CRISTINA

Thanks.

> PAUL

You're welcome.

Paul grabs a pen and paper from the glove compartment and writes down a number.

This is my cellphone number, just in case.

She puts the piece of paper in her sweatpants. She grabs her bag from the back seat and, as she is about to get out, Paul holds her by the elbow.

Wanna have lunch with me tomorrow?

She looks at Paul's hand and he lets go.

> CRISTINA

What for?

The question takes Paul by surprise, but he answers quickly.

> PAUL

So your kidneys won't hurt from eating alone.

She smiles: there is something about him that disarms her.

How about Lawrence's tomorrow at two? It's nearby.

> CRISTINA

OK, see you tomorrow.

Cristina gets out and closes the door.

119. INT. PAUL'S CAR — MOMENTS LATER

Paul drives. He reaches a stop light. Suddenly a sharp pain makes him bring his hand to his heart. He breathes with difficulty. He barely opens the car door in time to vomit.

The light turns green. The cars behind him honk their horns. Paul finishes vomiting. He closes the door and puts his hands on the steering wheel.

The driver behind him is honking furiously. Paul puts the car in gear and drives off.

120. EXT. STREET (CONTINUATION OF SCENE 65) — NIGHT

Laura sees a white cat a few feet away.

> LAURA
> (*out of shot*)
> Daddy, Daddy . . . a kitty . . .

The two girls walk over to it.

> MICHAEL
> (*out of shot*)
> Don't touch it . . . Laura, leave it . . .

The cat walks past them and the girls turn to look at it.

> OK, honey, I'll see you at home.

He hangs up. Lucio is clearing out leaves with a leaf blower. Michael and his daughters bump into him.

> LUCIO
> Good night, Mr Beck.

> MICHAEL
> Good night, Lucio . . . and don't forget to do the garden on Saturday.

> LUCIO
> No sir, I won't forget.

Michael and his daughters continue on their way. Laura keeps looking at Lucio, who smiles at her.

Michael and the girls walk away and Lucio continues with the leaf blower. Suddenly a silver Ford Lobo crosses the street at high speed. Lucio looks at it and goes back to his work.

Squealing brakes and a strong blow are heard. Lucio raises his eyes, stupefied. After a few seconds he runs towards the sound.

121. EXT. PRISON GATE — MORNING

At the foot of the steps is Marianne. She wears jeans, sunglasses and a comfortable blouse.

Jack and John walk through the main gate. Jack looks tired, dishevelled, with his beard grown out. He stops to look at the world to which he returns a free man. The sun blinds him and he lifts his hand to see better.

Marianne spots Jack, takes off her sunglasses and walks up the stairs towards him. Jack looks at her briefly and walks by without paying attention to her.

She closes her eyes, furious and humiliated.

> MARIANNE
> (*muttering*)
> Son of a bitch.

> JOHN
> It'll blow over, Marianne.

Jack keeps walking without slowing down. John runs, catches up with him and stops him.

> Where are you going?

Jack doesn't answer and keeps going. John cuts in again.

> Your children baked you a cake. They're waiting for you.

122. POINT OF VIEW PRISON GATE — CONTINUOUS

Marianne watches them talk from a distance, without hearing what they are saying. John leaves Jack and walks past her towards the car.

> JOHN
> I convinced him. He's coming with us.

> MARIANNE
> He's a fucking piece of shit . . .

John stops and then walks up to her.

JOHN

Jesus will show him the way to . . .

MARIANNE

Jesus? What the fuck does Jesus have to do with this, John?
Leave us alone with that. Goddammit!

Marianne turns around and heads towards the car.

123. INT. DOCTOR ROTHBERG'S OFFICE — AFTERNOON

*Rothberg, worried, looks at some echocardiograms. Paul watches him,
expectant.*

PAUL

Is there something wrong?

ROTHBERG
(*serious*)

Your body's rejecting the heart. That's why you're short of
breath and you've been vomiting so much.

PAUL

But it's been six months and I've felt more or less OK.

ROTHBERG

Sometimes it happens, sometimes it doesn't. Everybody
reacts differently; especially if you smoke.

Paul seems in disbelief; he is noticeably upset.

PAUL

What if we change the medications?

ROTHBERG

I'm going to be frank: the heart you're carrying will stop
working soon. I need to keep you in the hospital until we
find another heart.

*Paul is devastated by the news. He brings his hand to his forehead and
rubs it desperately.*

PAUL

You want me to wait for another heart?

86

ROTHBERG

We don't have any other choice . . .

PAUL

I can't wait for someone else to die while I'm locked in a
goddamn room again . . . I can't . . .

ROTHBERG

You're dangerously close to heart failure . . . Paul, you might
die a lot sooner than you think; two months at most . . .

Paul stands up and looks him straight in the eyes.

PAUL

Swear that you'll tell me the truth: if I'm put back in the
hospital, is there a chance I'll be saved?

ROTHBERG

I can't guarantee it, but if you don't come back to the
hospital you're condemning yourself to a terrible death:
your heart won't work any more and you'll die asphyxiated.
It's an awful death, Paul, you can't imagine it. At least here
we can help you to –

PAUL
(*interrupts brusquely*)
To die better? That's what you'll help me with? No thanks,
doctor, I'd rather die outside.

124. INT. JOHN'S CAR – DAY

*John drives, Jack sits next to him and in the back Marianne stares
out of the window. They are silent, tense.*

JACK
How much did you pay the lawyer?

He turns to Marianne waiting for an answer.

How much did the fucking monkey charge?

Marianne still doesn't answer. John breaks the silence.

JOHN
Enough.

JACK

How much is enough?

MARIANNE
(*annoyed*)
Enough so that your kids can remember your fucking face.

Pause.

And if you keep asking stupid questions I'm getting out on
the next corner.

Jack doesn't say anything else, turns around. The three remain silent.

125. INT. LIVING ROOM, JACK'S HOUSE — DAY

*Freddy and Gina draw on the floor. They hear a noise and the door
opens. Both children raise their heads. Jack walks into the house. Gina
runs to greet him. Freddy gets up and, withdrawn, goes to a corner.*

GINA

Daddy . . . Daddy . . .

*Jack bends down to kiss her. Out of the corner of his eye he watches
his son staring at the floor.*

GINA

What did you bring us?

JACK

A kiss.

GINA

You didn't bring me a present?

*He bends down to kiss them again. Gina shows him the cake on the
table.*

We made you a cake.

JACK

Thank you, sweethearts.

Marianne intervenes.

MARIANNE
Freddy put the icing on it . . .

Jack turns to look at his son.

JACK
Aren't you going to say hello?

The boy walks up to Jack without looking at him, hugs him coldly and walks away again.

Marianne points at some drawings on the wall.

MARIANNE
Freddy drew those for you.

Freddy shyly looks up at his father and then looks down again. Gina points at some other drawings hanging on the doors.

GINA
And I drew those ones.

Jack looks at them, touched.

JACK
Thank you . . .

Jack starts to choke up.

GINA
What's the matter, Daddy?

JACK
Nothing, sweetie, nothing . . .

He strokes her head, tries to smile and cannot. He turns around, looks for Marianne and hugs her. He buries his face in her shoulder.

126. INT. RESTAURANT — DAY

Paul and Cristina are sitting in a very chic, modern restaurant with large open windows and a terrace open to the street. There are barely three occupied tables.

Their table is just at the edge between the inner part of the restaurant and the terrace with the open window.

Paul drinks red wine and Cristina holds a glass of vodka with ice in her hand. She looks slightly tipsy. On the table are plates with the remains of their dessert.

CRISTINA

Advanced math? That's what you teach?

PAUL

Yep, that.

Cristina gives her vodka a long drink. He watches her.

CRISTINA

And what do you teach them?

PAUL

That numbers aren't cold, that numbers express life. That numbers sometimes are an order, sometimes a chaos. That there's a hidden number in every act of life, in every manifestation of the universe, that there's a number screaming to tell us something. That a number . . .

Paul, who has been getting increasingly excited with each word, suddenly stops and looks at Cristina.

Am I boring you?

CRISTINA

No, not at all . . .

PAUL

I teach them that a number is always the door to a mystery bigger than us and that there's no bigger mystery than two people meeting . . . Do you know who Eugenio Montejo is?

CRISTINA

No, who is he?

PAUL

A poet from Venezuela, my favourite one. He has a poem that says: 'The earth turned to bring us closer, turned on itself and in us until it finally brought us together in this dream.'

He remains serious, meditative. He turns to look at her.

So many things have to happen for two people to meet.
(*A beat.*) That's what mathematics is about.

Paul pulls out a cigarette and lights it. Almost immediately, a waiter walks over to them.

WAITER

I'm sorry, sir, but you can't smoke in this area.

Paul points at the smoke going out of the open window.

PAUL

But the smoke goes out the window. Besides, there's no one here.

WAITER

I'm sorry sir, you can only smoke on the terrace.

PAUL
(*to Cristina*)
Do you mind if we change tables?

CRISTINA

No.

They move to the adjoining table on the terrace open to the street, taking their wine glasses with them. The waiter interrupts again.

WAITER

I'm sorry, but state law prohibits the consumption of alcoholic beverages on the terrace.

Paul closes his eyes as if to say 'You're not serious.'

PAUL
(*to Cristina*)
There are limits to the mysteries that maths can answer.

He turns to the other table and drinks his wine, turns around again and smokes on the terrace. Cristina laughs, amused.

127. EXT. RESTAURANT — DAY

They head towards Paul's car. When he is about to open the door, Cristina stops for a moment.

CRISTINA

Do you mind if we walk?

128. EXT. STREET — MOMENTS LATER

They walk down the street. The day is overcast and Cristina has her hands inside her coat.

PAUL

How many years have you been swimming?

CRISTINA

Oh, for years.

PAUL

Doesn't it bore you?

CRISTINA

No. It's what makes me feel best. The day I don't swim
I feel lost and if I didn't swim . . . (*Pauses, thinks.*) I think
I'd go crazy.

She turns to look at him and smiles sadly. Paul tries to change the subject.

PAUL

Do you compete?

CRISTINA

Yes, when I'm sure I'll win.

Both smile. They arrive at her house.

PAUL

Goodbye.

CRISTINA

Thanks for lunch.

They wave goodbye. Cristina is about to walk in when she suddenly turns to Paul.

Do you want to come in and I'll give you your jacket?

129. INT. MOTEL ROOM — DAY/EARLY MORNING

Paul, dressed, is sitting on the bed watching Cristina sleep (dressed in black shorts and a T-shirt as in Scene 106 where she drinks tequila). He caresses her, but she remains inert.

Paul gets up and sees the almost empty bottle of tequila on the night-stand. Then he looks at Cristina asleep again, grabs the revolver, tucks it in his pants and leaves.

130. EXT. PAUL'S CAR/HIGHWAY MOTEL — LATER

Paul's car is parked in the motel parking lot, facing the rooms. Watching from his car, Paul smokes with the door open and sweats profusely. In his lap is the .38 Smith and Wesson. He opens the cylinder, makes sure the bullets are in place and closes it again.

He sees Jack leave his room through the windshield and quickly tucks the gun into his waist. He lets Jack walk a few steps and gets out of the car.

131. EXT. DESERT ROAD — CONTINUOUS

Jack walks down the edge of the road. Paul follows him some ten yards behind. He suddenly quickens his pace, pulls out the gun and aims it at Jack's head.

Jack turns around and is startled.

> PAUL
Walk.

He points at a path into the desert. Jack stands still. Paul puts the gun between Jack's eyes.

I said walk.

He points at the path again.

And put your hands on your head.

They reach an isolated clearing. Jack walks with his hands on his head. Paul, aiming at Jack, signals a spot between two mesquites. Both look very nervous.

> PAUL

Stand over there.

> JACK

I don't have any money.

> PAUL

Shut the fuck up.

Jack gulps. The sun shines out between the shrubs.

> JACK

Are you going to kill me?

Paul points the gun at Jack's face.

> PAUL

I said shut the fuck up! (*A beat.*) Get on your knees and take off your shoes.

Paul looks as if he is about to shoot. The revolver shakes in his hand. He sweats and is pale.

> JACK

Do I get on my knees or do I take my shoes off?

> PAUL

Take off your shoes.

Jack takes off one of his shoes and Paul signals for him to throw it to one side. Jack does, Paul grabs the shoe and tosses it away.

Jack starts taking off the other shoe.

Not that one, leave it on . . . Get on your knees and put your hands on your head.

Jack obeys.

You shouldn't have done it! Goddammit! Y-o-u s-h-o-u-l-d-n-'t . . .

Jack looks up; Paul still points.

JACK

Done what?

PAUL

Don't look at me.

He looks tense, about to shoot. Jack lowers his head.

JACK

What do you want?

*Paul doesn't answer. Jack raises his head and looks him in the eyes.
Paul gets even more nervous.*

PAUL

Close your eyes . . . Close them, goddammit!

*Jack does not comply. Paul squats, grabs some dirt and throws it in his
eyes. Jack opens and closes them with difficulty.*

I said close them.

Suddenly Paul stretches out his arm and fires three times.

133. INT. ROOM JACK'S HOUSE – AFTERNOON

*Jack is sitting on the bed dressed as in Scene 121 when he gets out of
jail. Marianne, before him, bends down and kisses him on the mouth.
She moves back and takes off her blouse and brassiere. She has a
small tattoo on her left shoulder.*

*She starts to unbutton his shirt and to kiss him on the neck with a
certain anxiety.*

MARIANNE

I missed you, I missed you so much . . .

*She is increasingly aroused. Jack, after being distant, is turned on,
takes Marianne's pants off and gets naked.*

*He turns Marianne face down and starts fucking her roughly and
with no amorous concessions. She seems as if she is on the edge of
enjoying or suffering.*

95

Suddenly Jack stops, hugs her from behind and starts crying. She turns to kiss him, but he will not stop crying.

JACK
(*almost unable to speak*)
She looked me in the eyes.

MARIANNE
What are you talking about?

JACK
One of the girls that I killed, she looked me in the eyes and wanted to tell me something and I didn't do anything to help her . . .

He hugs her forcefully, as if here were going to break her, crying. She cries with him.

134. INT. LIVING ROOM, CRISTINA'S HOUSE — DAY

Paul and Cristina enter the living room. He walks in shyly.

CRISTINA
Do you want something to drink?

PAUL
No thanks.

CRISTINA
Well, at least have a glass of wine.

PAUL
I'll have some coffee.

CRISTINA
Sugar?

PAUL
Yeah, two sugars.

Cristina walks out. Paul looks around the living room. On a table he sees a photograph of Michael and Cristina holding their girls. He picks it up and looks at it. He stares at Michael's face.

He sighs and puts the portrait back. It is obvious that looking at it has upset him.

Cristina returns with a coffee in one hand and a glass of vodka in the other. She finds Paul pale and unsettled. She sets the drinks on the table.

CRISTINA

Are you alright?

PAUL

I got a little dizzy.

CRISTINA

Do you need anything?

Paul stands up.

PAUL

I'm sorry, but I'm not feeling well. I'd better leave. I need to lie down.

CRISTINA
(disconcerted)

OK.

Cristina's demeanour is surly again. Paul's sudden departure seems to have ruined the atmosphere.

135. INT. ENTRANCE, CRISTINA'S HOUSE – CONTINUOUS

They are standing in front of the door.

PAUL

Can I see you again?

CRISTINA
(aggressive)

What for?

Paul swallows nervously and looks her in the eyes.

PAUL

I like you a lot, Cristina. It's been a long time since I liked someone this much.

Cristina is disconcerted. She lowers her head, ashamed.

CRISTINA

I'm a married woman.

PAUL

I figured.

Paul tries to lift her head by touching her chin, but Cristina moves away.

CRISTINA

Goodbye.

Paul doesn't know what to say. Now he is the one that is disconcerted.

PAUL

'Bye.

Without shaking hands, they part with a soft nod of the head. Paul turns around and leaves.

136. INT. RELIGIOUS CENTER — EVENING

The congregation is gathered at a ceremony. Among them are Jack and his family.

JOHN

Jesus is the light . . .

EVERYONE

Jesus is the light . . .

Jack barely mumbles the phrases every now and then. Some members burst again into spontaneous 'amens' as in Scene 15.

MEMBERS

Amen . . . Amen . . .

JOHN

Jesus is hope . . .

EVERYONE

Jesus is hope . . .

Several members of the congregation turn to look at Jack and whisper to each other. He spots a few glances his way, among them the boy from Scene 4 with whom he played Jenga, who watches him somewhat mockingly.

JOHN
Jesus is the water that quenches our thirst.

EVERYONE
Jesus is the water that quenches our thirst.

MEMBERS
Amen . . . Amen . . .

JOHN
Jesus is forgiveness.

EVERYONE
Jesus is forgiveness.

Jack looks at them out of the corner of his eye for a few seconds and tries unsuccessfully to pray.

137. DOCTOR'S OFFICE – EVENING

Mary is sitting before the doctor's desk. He watches her reticently.

GYNAECOLOGIST
Are you entirely sure?

Mary nods.

And your husband agrees?

Mary remains pensive and takes some time to answer.

MARY
Yes.

GYNAECOLOGIST
We'll operate this Thursday at seven a.m. Remember not to eat the night before . . .

He starts writing out a prescription.

. . . and take one of these every twelve hours until the surgery . . .

He hands her the prescription. Mary takes it and puts it away in her purse mechanically.

138. INT. ROOM HIGHWAY MOTEL — NIGHT

Cristina sleeps in a T-shirt and shorts. We hear someone cough and breath agitatedly. Cristina wakes up, sits on the bed and realises the bathroom light is on.

139. INT. BATHROOM, HIGHWAY MOTEL ROOM — CONTINUOUS

She gets up and goes to the bathroom. She finds Paul sitting on the floor against the tiling on the wall, coughing and breathing with difficulty. He looks pale and limp.

Cristina squats next to him, worried.

> CRISTINA
> What's the matter?

Paul wets his dry lips. He has trouble talking.

> PAUL
> I feel terrible.

Cristina wipes the sweat off his forehead with a caress. She sees three cigarette butts in the toilet.

> CRISTINA
> You're smoking too much. I don't think it's very good for your heart.

> PAUL
> This has nothing to do with smoking.

Cristina keeps stroking his forehead, a little bit anxious. She grabs one of his hands.

> CRISTINA
> I'm going to take you to a doctor . . .

She looks very anguished and she lovingly kisses his forehead repeatedly. Paul hugs her.

PAUL

No, it'll pass . . .

They remain in each other's arms on the bathroom floor.

140. INT. JACK'S HOUSE — EVENING

Jack, Marianne and Freddy watch television in the living room while Gina makes drawings on the coffee table.

MARIANNE
(*to Jack*)
Brown called to say he found you a job as a caddy at the WD club.

JACK
I'll call him tomorrow.

They go back to watching the TV show. Gina finishes her drawing and shows it to her father.

GINA
Look, Daddy, I drew a zoo.

Jack looks at it. The girl stands next to him.

These are the zebras and these are the lions.

FREDDY
How can you draw a zoo if you've never been to one?

GINA
I see them on TV.

JACK
Hey! Stop fighting . . . (*to Gina*) It's very pretty.

Gina goes back to the table to draw.

MARIANNE
The lawyer also called to remind you you have to go sign on Monday.

Jack nods as he watches TV, completely gone. Marianne holds his hand and strokes it.

MARIANNE

Do you want me to go to the church with you again?

Jack refuses again. He changes the channel several times until he stops on a documentary on animals.

Gina, without raising her eyes from the sketchpad, asks her father:

GINA

Daddy, in school they say you killed two girls and their daddy. Is that true?

Both parents answer contrarily in unison.

MARIANNE

No.

JACK

Yes.

They both look at each other for a few seconds. Freddy stops watching television to look at them.

FREDDY

Yes, he killed them.

The boy's words disturb Jack completely. For a few seconds he does not know what to say.

MARIANNE

It was an accident, sweetie.

Jack looks at her harshly. Gina remains pensive for a few seconds and keeps drawing. Without much fuss, Jack gets up and goes to his room.

Marianne glares at Freddy, who can only lower his head.

141. INT. ROOM, PAUL'S APARTMENT — NIGHT

Paul and Mary sleep. We suddenly hear a noise. Both wake up in a haze. Paul gets up, turns on the light, rummages through his clothes and pulls out a cellular phone.

PAUL

Hello . . .

No answer.

Hello . . .

> CRISTINA
> (*out of shot*)

Paul?

> PAUL

Yes, who is this?

> CRISTINA
> (*out of shot*)

Cristina.

Paul, bewildered, leaves the room.

142. INT. LIVING ROOM, PAUL'S APARTMENT − CONTINUOUS

> CRISTINA
> (*out of shot*)

Did I wake you?

> PAUL

No, it's OK.

Mary walks out, leans on a wall and listens to him.

> CRISTINA
> (*out of shot*)

Could you come to my house?

> PAUL

Is something wrong?

> CRISTINA

No, I just want you to come . . . (*A beat.*) If you can . . . if you want to . . .

Paul looks at a clock on the wall. It is two a.m.

> PAUL

I'll be right over.

He hangs up and holds the cellphone in his hand. He heads towards the room. Mary follows.

143. INT. ROOM, PAUL'S APARTMENT — CONTINUOUS

Paul grabs his clothes and starts to get dressed.

> MARY
> It's two in the morning. What, or who, have you gotten into?

> PAUL
> I won't be long.

He finishes getting dressed, grabs a jacket and heads towards the door. Mary steps in front of him.

> MARY
> Where are you going?

> PAUL
> I said I won't be long.

> MARY
> Exactly where and with whom are you going?

Paul doesn't answer. She faces him.

> I thought you'd change after the transplant.

> PAUL
> I thought you'd change if you got pregnant. But look: neither of us changed . . . I'll be back later.

Paul says no more, walks around Mary and leaves.

144. INT. JACK'S ROOM — NIGHT

Marianne sleeps. Jack stands next to the bed dressed in blue jeans and a leather jacket. He bends down and kisses Marianne on the forehead. She shifts.

Jack looks at her for a few seconds, grabs a small suitcase from near the door and leaves.

145. INT. LIVING ROOM, JACK'S HOUSE — CONTINUOUS

Jack puts the suitcase on the floor and stares, in the dark, at the picture of him receiving the keys to his truck.

He turns around and walks towards the back door. He opens it, walks out and comes back in with a cage with a hamster in it.

146. INT. CHILDREN'S ROOM, JACK'S HOUSE — CONTINUOUS

Jack walks into the room and puts the cage on the nightstand between the two beds. He walks towards Gina's bed and sees she is uncovered. He pulls the comforter over her and kisses her on the cheek.

He then does the same with Freddy. He kisses him and leaves.

147. EXT. JACK'S HOUSE — CONTINUOUS

Jack walks out of the house carrying the small suitcase.

148. EXT. PUBLIC SERVICE CLINIC — NIGHT/DAWN

Jack hurriedly parks in front of the 'Emergency' sign. He gets out and opens the back door. Paul is bleeding on Cristina's lap.

A very young doctor and a night guard walk up to them.

> JACK
>
> Please, help us . . .

> YOUNG DOCTOR
> (*frightened*)
>
> What happened?

> JACK
>
> He's been shot in the chest . . .

> YOUNG DOCTOR
>
> How long has he been . . .

Cristina, from inside the car, begs.

> CRISTINA
>
> For fuck's sake, he's dying . . .

The doctor looks at Paul on the verge of death.

> YOUNG DOCTOR
>
> I'll go get a stretcher.

He runs inside the hospital. The night guard looks into the car. Cristina looks at him and doesn't say anything. She strokes Paul's head. He breathes in hoarse, deep gasps.

Suddenly, Jack turns to the night guard.

> JACK
>
> I shot him.

The night guard draws his gun and points it at Jack.

> NIGHT GUARD
>
> Turn around and put your hands behind your neck.

Jack does so. Cristina stares astonished at Jack. While the guard pulls out his radio, and without moving the gun away from Jack, he asks his base to call the police.

> Attention, base . . . call the police . . . it's urgent . . . call the police . . .

149. EXT. CRISTINA'S HOUSE – NIGHT

Paul rings the doorbell. Cristina opens, slightly drunk. Paul is taken aback by seeing her like this.

She is wearing a lead-blue dress, the same one as in Scene 1.

150. INT. ENTRANCE, CRISTINA'S HOUSE – CONTINUOUS

Paul walks inside and closes the door. They look at each other without speaking for a moment. She looks very anxious.

> PAUL
>
> Hi.

Cristina doesn't answer. The words seem to simmer in her head, but she cannot find a way to say them.

> Are you OK?

She looks him in the eyes, lowers her gaze for a moment and looks at him again.

CRISTINA

You know, you kept me thinking all day. I haven't spoken to anyone for months and I barely know you and I already need to talk to you . . . (*A beat.*) And there's something the more I think about the less I understand: why the hell did you tell me you liked me?

He moves closer to her and strokes her hair. She moves away.

Answer me, because I didn't like you saying that at all.

Cristina seems as if she is about to crack. Her gestures are abrupt. She shifts her gaze from one place to another.

You can't just walk up to a woman you barely know and tell her you like her. Y-o-u c-a-n-'t. You don't know what she's going through, what she's feeling.

Cristina stops and closes her eyes. She mumbles some unintelligible phrases. Paul moves closer to stroke her hair again. She submits, opens her eyes and looks at him directly.

I'm not married, you know. I'm not anything in this world. I'm just not anything . . .

Cristina cannot hold on any longer and, broken, hugs him. Paul strokes her head, trying to calm her down. She raises her face slightly and moves away from him. She looks at him, raises her hands and starts kissing him on the mouth.

Paul doesn't know whether to answer the kiss or not, but goes along anyway. They kiss with increasing intensity.

The kissing leads to stroking. Without ceasing to kiss and touch each other, they lean on the wall.

Cristina kisses him desperately, slightly out of control. Paul moves away from her and grabs her hands. Cristina tries to kiss him, but he stops her.

PAUL

Cristina, I want you to know something.

Cristina, still agitated from the excitement, tries to get near him, but Paul stops her again.

Cristina, listen.

Cristina moves back, ready to listen.

I have Michael's heart.

Cristina looks at him, stunned.

I had his heart transplanted May the second at St George's Hospital . . .

Cristina's face starts to harden.

CRISTINA
(*in a low voice*)
Get out of my house.

Paul tries to grab her by the hand and she pulls away.

PAUL
Cristina I . . . tried to . . .

She looks at him furiously.

CRISTINA
How dare you come here . . . Get out.

Paul tries to say something else, but Cristina lets fly a right cross to his jaw that he cannot dodge. She tries to hit him again, but he holds her hands.

PAUL
I'm here for a reason . . . can't you see?

Cristina breaks loose violently.

CRISTINA
Why didn't you tell me before? Goddammit, why?

Paul confronts her.

PAUL
Cristina . . . you . . .

She pushes him towards the door.

CRISTINA
Get the fuck out . . . you make me sick. Get out.

She keeps pushing him. Paul raises his hands in surrender. He opens the door and leaves.

Cristina slams the door shut, leans on the wall and starts to cry disconsolately.

151. INT. LOCAL COUNTY PRECINCT — NIGHT

Jack is sitting on a metal chair in a small precinct office. He is cuffed before the county sheriff (thirty-seven), and watched by two guards.

> SHERIFF
> At what time did the shooting take place?

> JACK
> Around seven p.m.

> SHERIFF
> What was your relationship with Mr Paul Rivers?

> JACK
> I didn't know him. He came to threaten to kill me.

> SHERIFF
> And what did you do?

> JACK
> Nothing. He left.

> SHERIFF
> And then?

> JACK
> I went looking for him.

> SHERIFF
> What for?

> JACK
> To kill him before he killed me.

> SHERIFF
> And then you shot him?

JACK

Yes, sir.

The officer stands up and quickly looks at some papers.

SHERIFF

Your statement contradicts the statement made by Ms Cristina Williams.

Jack looks at him without saying a word.

152. INT. ROOM, CRISTINA'S HOUSE — MORNING

Cristina is woken up by the light coming through the window. She is asleep with the same lead-blue dress from Scene 150, where she throws Paul out.

She sits up lazily on the bed and looks at the clock: 7:02 a.m. She rubs her forehead as if she were hung-over.

She stands up, goes to the curtains to close them. She discovers Paul's car parked in front of her house.

153. EXT. CRISTINA'S HOUSE — MOMENTS LATER

Cristina walks out, barefoot. She is wearing the lead-blue dress. She looks gaunt, with swollen eyes.

She heads towards Paul's car, looks through the window and finds him sleeping inside. She steps back a few paces as if to leave, turns around and looks in again.

She knocks on the window. Paul doesn't wake up. She insists. Paul rubs his eyes and unlocks the doors. He looks awful: tired and filthy. She opens the door and gets in.

154. INT. PAUL'S CAR — CONTINUOUS

PAUL

Good morning.

Cristina is still angry, confused, hurt. She is quiet for a long time.

CRISTINA

Why did you look for me?

PAUL

Because I needed to.

She turns and looks at him harshly.

CRISTINA

You don't know how much I fucking hate being looked for out of pity . . .

PAUL

No, that's not it . . .

CRISTINA

Then why?

They remain silent for a while.

PAUL

I was sick, Cristina. Very sick. I was dying when I got Michael's heart . . . He saved my life.

He stops for a moment. From the dashboard, he grabs a pack of cigarettes, takes one out and lights it. He opens the window and blows out the smoke into the cold morning air.

I looked every way I could to find out who had given me his heart. I even hired a private investigator. And then I found out who it was and how he and your daughters had died. (*A beat.*) It's painful for me to know how I got this heart.

He is pensive again. Cristina listens quietly.

I couldn't sleep, I couldn't stop thinking that I had to give something in exchange for his heart. I rang your doorbell several times, looking for you. I wanted to help in some way, to thank you for what I'd received. But I didn't find you. (*A beat.*) The day I saw you I was too attracted to you. And now I can't be away from you any more . . . I really can't . . .

He looks moved. She looks at the floor and then at him again.

CRISTINA
You scare me, you know that?

PAUL
There's nothing to be afraid of . . . (*He points at his chest.*)
I've got a good heart.

*He smiles absently. They are silent for a long time. Paul takes
Cristina's left hand and puts it on his chest.*

(*Joking.*) This heart never stopped loving you.

He smiles again, now sadly.

I'm also very scared.

*Cristina looks at him, surprised: he is a man that says and does
strange things. She opens her hand and feels his chest for a few
moments and then rests her ear on it.*

*She listens for a few moments and then starts to cry softly. Paul holds
her and delicately kisses her on the forehead. He then lowers his head
and kisses her on the mouth.*

155. INT. PAUL'S APARTMENT — EVENING

*Mary is sitting alone in the living room, sad and pensive. She stands
up and opens a closet. She pulls out the jar in which Paul's heart
floats. She holds it up to the light. The heart bounces against the glass.*

156. INT. CRISTINA'S BEDROOM — DAY

*Paul and Cristina are naked on the bed, kissing. On the chair is his
leather jacket and on the floor is Cristina's lead-blue dress (the same
from Scene 1).*

*She looks him in the eyes and caresses his face. They start to make
love. She holds him tightly and starts to cry. She cries and cries,
shivering.*

*Paul notices she is crying. He moves away to watch her. He tries to say
something, but she pulls him towards her and kisses him, still crying,
while they continue to make love.*

157. INT. DINING ROOM JACK'S HOUSE — EVENING

Marianne helps her kids with their homework in the dining room.

> MARIANNE
> (*to Gina*)
> What's five times seven?

Gina starts to count with her fingers.

> Think about it; don't count with your fingers.

Gina stops using her fingers, but it is obvious that she is looking for something to count with.

The phone rings and Marianne goes to answer.

> Hello . . .

Nobody answers. A radio playing Tex-Mex music is heard.

158. INTERCUT INT. LOBBY, HIGHWAY MOTEL — CONTINUOUS

Jack is on the phone at the motel's chipped reception desk. It is a simple lobby, with worn sofas and tacky imitation paintings.

A skinny woman (fifty) with dyed hair, listens to the radio sitting on a bench on the other side of the counter. Jack listens to Marianne.

> MARIANNE
> (*out of shot*)
> Hello . . . hello . . .

> JACK
> Marianne . . .

> MARIANNE
> (*out of shot*)
> Jack, where are you?

> JACK
> I'm where I have to be . . .

> MARIANNE
> (*out of shot*)
> Are you sure you're OK?

There is a long pause. Jack takes a while in answering.

> JACK
> I can't look my children in the eyes, I can't look you in the
> eyes.

> MARIANNE
> (*out of shot*)
> Jack, the kids love you, I love you. We'll go to wherever you
> are . . .

> JACK
> No. What happened had to happen and whatever happens
> has to happen.

> MARIANNE
> (*out of shot*)
> What?

> JACK
> God writes against us and there's nothing we can do to
> erase it. We can't escape him . . . we can't . . .

Crying is heard on the other end of the phone.

> MARIANNE
> (*out of shot*)
> Jack, what are you talking about?

> JACK
> God laughs at us and squeezes us with his burning hands . . .

> MARIANNE
> Jack, please . . .

> JACK
> It's in his hands, not mine . . .

*Jack hangs up the receiver on the old-fashioned cream-coloured phone
and remains pensive, breathing agitatedly.*

159. INT. HALLWAY, RURAL PUBLIC SERVICE CLINIC – NIGHT/DAWN

*Cristina is sitting in a row of orange plastic chairs in a humble clinic
with few people.*

A female doctor in a white gown walks up to her.

> DOCTOR
> Are you a relative of Paul Rivers's?

Cristina stands up.

> CRISTINA
> How is he?

> DOCTOR
> We're doing everything we can to save his life. We've already
> called an ambulance to get him to the hospital. (*A beat.*)
> Right now we urgently need units of B-positive blood.

> CRISTINA
> I'm O-positive. Will that work?

160. INT. CUBICLE, RURAL PUBLIC SERVICE CLINIC —
MOMENTS LATER

*Cristina is sitting in a small cubicle with her left arm stretched out
towards a nurse, who prepares a needle.*

> NURSE
> Have you ever had any infectious diseases such as hepatitis
> or HIV?

*Cristina shakes her head. She watches as the nurse ties a tourniquet to
her arm.*

> Are you using any medication or is there anything that
> would prevent you from donating blood?

*Cristina takes some time to answer. Upon seeing this, the nurse stops
the procedure and looks her in the eyes.*

> CRISTINA
> No.

> NURSE
> Are you sure?

> CRISTINA
> Yes.

NURSE

Open and close your fist several times.

Cristina does and the nurse sticks the needle into her vein and she small jar starts filling with blood.

161. INT. CRISTINA'S ROOM (BEGINNING SCENE 1) — DAY

Paul and Cristina are lying in bed. Their clothes are strewn about the room as in Scene 1.

Paul wakes up and looks at Cristina asleep next to him. He sits on the mattress and lights a cigarette. On the nightstand beside him he sees a book, a case for glasses, and a male wristwatch.

It is obvious this was Michael's nightstand. He takes the book: it is Cruising Paradise *by Sam Shepard. He leafs through it and discovers a Polaroid photograph of Michael and Cristina hugging and smiling.*

Paul studies it and puts it back between the pages. He closes the book, grabs the case and takes out the glasses. He puts them on, looks through them and then puts them back in their place.

He opens the nightstand drawer. Inside is a small plastic bag with cocaine and some R-2 pills beside it. He moistens his finger, rubs some coke on his gums and then puts the bag back in the drawer.

He turns to Cristina and sadly looks at her naked back. He runs one of his fingers down her back without ceasing to look at her.

Cristina shifts position without waking up. Paul blows out smoke and brings his hand to his forehead, worried.

162. INT. POLICE STATION — EVENING

Jack is sitting before an empty desk. The sheriff arrives, sits down and places some papers on the desk.

SHERIFF

You're free to leave for lack of evidence.

JACK

But I've confessed.

Your story doesn't check out. It contradicts our
investigation and Ms Cristina Williams's statement.

He hands him a document.

Sign here.

Jack takes the paper and signs it.

JACK
And what if I really am guilty?

SHERIFF
It won't be the first time it happens. You're free to go.

163. INT. DINING ROOM CRISTINA'S HOUSE — DAY

Cristina, Claudia and their father eat. They look tense.

FATHER
(*to Cristina*)
Could you pass the mashed potatoes?

Cristina passes them over. Claudia intercepts the bowl.

CLAUDIA
(*to her father*)
I'll serve you some.

Claudia looks at her sister reproachfully and serves her father.

FATHER
I went to the movies last week.

CLAUDIA
How was it?

FATHER
So, so. By the way, I saw Liz at the movies. She says hi.

CLAUDIA
Which Liz?

FATHER
My friend from work. Remember?

117

Cristina, absent from the conversation, raises her eyes towards her father.

CRISTINA
(*sarcastic*)

Your friend?

FATHER
(*upset*)

She was just my friend.

CRISTINA

It's just that she slept in your room so much, she and the . . . what were the names of the other six 'friends'?

CLAUDIA

Don't talk to my father like that.

CRISTINA

I'm just telling the truth.

CLAUDIA

It wasn't his fault that Mom died and left him alone.

FATHER

Claudia, stay out of this.

CRISTINA

Are you trying to say that what happened to me is my fault?

Claudia stares at her fixedly.

CLAUDIA

No, not yours. And not Dad's. But Jack Jordan, who's guilty of everything, is going to walk tomorrow. And that doesn't seem to bother you.

CRISTINA

I don't give a shit about him.

CLAUDIA

You would if you knew what the son of a bitch did that night.

CRISTINA
(*disturbed*)

What are you talking about?

CLAUDIA

You'd know what I'm talking about if you'd at least read
Lucio's declaration, the kid that does the garden, the only
witness to the accident.

FATHER

Enough, Claudia.

CRISTINA

There were no witnesses.

CLAUDIA

Oh no? Keep hiding, Cristina, keep getting drunk and
drugged until reality seeps into your life like moisture and
cracks you into pieces . . .

FATHER

Stop it . . . that's enough . . .

*Cristina is stunned. Claudia looks at her harshly, conscious of the fact
that she just won a long-awaited moral victory.*

164. INT. LIVING ROOM PAUL'S APARTMENT – AFTERNOON

*Paul walks into the house. He is dressed in the same clothes from
Scene 150 when he went to see Cristina. He sees a suitcase in the living
room and several things out of place. He hears noises in his room and
he goes to see.*

165. INT. PAUL'S ROOM – AFTERNOON

*Paul stands at the door and finds Mary packing clothes into another
suitcase. She turns quickly to look at Paul and then goes on packing.*

PAUL

What are you doing?

*Mary doesn't answer, concentrated on her task. She finishes folding a
blouse and turns to look at him.*

MARY

Taking my things to my apartment. (*A beat.*) You've been
lost for too many days, don't you think? You prick.

Paul stares at the clothes on the bed as if he will find an answer there and turns to look at her.

> PAUL
>
> I don't want to fight, Mary. I want this to end well.

> MARY
>
> You think ending well means disappearing for a few days? (*A beat.*) You just waited till you got better to tell me to fuck off.

> PAUL
>
> Mary, this can't go on any more.

> MARY
>
> Really?

Mary goes to the closet and pulls out a mound of clothes which she stuffs into the suitcase unfolded.

> Everything would have been different if we'd had a baby.

> PAUL
>
> That's not the problem.

Mary turns to look at him challengingly.

> MARY
>
> Of course it is, but I'm going to solve it my way. I will have surgery and I will be inseminated with your child, with or without you.

> PAUL
>
> What for?

> MARY
>
> Because I want to.

> PAUL
>
> Mary, I won't authorise it.

> MARY
>
> Oh no? You already did. I have a signed copy of your authorisation to use your semen.

She closes the suitcase and carries it towards the door.

>Would you excuse me?

Paul won't let her past.

PAUL

>What do you gain?

MARY

>I get what I want. You decide if you come looking for me
>or not.

She goes to the door. Paul moves aside and she walks away.

166. EXT. STREET – AFTERNOON

*Lucio is tending a garden. Cristina arrives and stands next to him. He
turns to greet her.*

LUCIO

>Good afternoon.

Cristina does not answer his greeting. She stares at him fixedly.

CRISTINA

>Lucio, did you see the accident where my family died?

LUCIO

>Yes, Miss Cristina.

CRISTINA

>Why didn't you tell me?

LUCIO

>I thought you knew. I told the police everything I saw.

Lucio is nervous.

CRISTINA

>What happened?

Lucio gulps and starts talking into the floor.

LUCIO

>They were about to cross the street and a truck . . .

Lucio stops. He has trouble going on.

> The man hit them very hard and he got out to see what happened. He stood there for a while, looking at them, without doing anything, and then ran to his truck and left them in the street.

It hurts Cristina to hear this. She can barely breathe.

> Then I ran to try and help them. Mr Beck and Katie were still alive. I tried to help Katie, but she started to moan horribly. I shouted for help and there wasn't anyone and, and . . . I did what I could, I swear . . .

His jaw shakes. Cristina stretches out her hand, caresses him lightly, turns around and leaves, holding in her tears.

167. EXT. SODA FOUNTAIN — AFTERNOON

Cristina walks down the street where the soda fountain is (the same as Scene 2, where Michael and his daughters went for the last time).

She stops in front of the entrance, cups her hands around her eyes and peers in.

168. INT. SODA FOUNTAIN — CONTINUOUS

The place is half-empty, with only a few clients. It contrasts with the clamour of the night of the accident.

169. EXT. SODA FOUNTAIN — CONTINUOUS

Cristina, greatly distressed, walks away from the door and looks into the street. She starts walking.

170. EXT. STREET CORNER (ACCIDENT) — CONTINUOUS

Cristina arrives at the corner where her family was run over. She looks both ways, steps off the sidewalk and crouches over the pavement. She touches it softly with her hand. She closes her eyes and puts her chin on her chest.

She stands up and opens her eyes. People walk around her: a man walks his dog, a grandmother walks hand in hand with her granddaughter, cars pass.

171. INT. CRISTINA'S ROOM — EVENING

Cristina is in her room, sitting on her bed. She grabs her cellphone and presses a button. Her old messages are heard.

> FATHER
> (*out of shot*)
> Sweetie, I was just calling to see if you wanted to have lunch next week . . . call me . . .

She presses a button and listens to the next message.

> MICHAEL
> (*out of shot*)
> Hey, honey, we're on our way home. If you need me to pick up anything on the way, give me a call on my cellphone.

> LAURA
> (*out of shot*)
> Daddy, Daddy . . . a kitty . . .

> MICHAEL
> (*out of shot*)
> Don't touch it . . . Laura, leave it . . . OK, honey, I'll see you at home.

Cristina breathes deeply, presses a button and listens again.

> Hey, honey, we're on our way home. If you need me to pick up anything on the way, give me a call on my cellphone.

> LAURA
> (*out of shot*)
> Daddy, Daddy . . . a kitty . . .

> MICHAEL
> (*out of shot*)
> Don't touch it . . . Laura, leave it . . . OK, honey, I'll see you at home.

Cristina lowers her head, rests the cellphone on her thigh and starts to cry quietly.

172. INT. JACK'S ROOM, HIGHWAY MOTEL – AFTERNOON

Jack (dressed as he was in Scene 132 when Paul shot at him) is sitting on his bed, alone, drunk and wretched. He drinks from a bottle of cheap rum.

Several objects surround him: photographs of his children, of Marianne, a small cross, a dirty glass.

He puts the bottle on a table and looks at himself in the mirror. He looks at the 'Jesus loves you' tattoo on his left forearm. He examines it for a long time.

He takes a knife, opens it, breathes deeply and starts to carve at the tattoo, trying to remove it. He bleeds profusely but does not stop until his forearm is in tatters.

He throws the knife away and stretches out his left arm, letting the blood drip onto the floor.

173. EXT. HALLWAY HIGHWAY MOTEL – LATER

Jack walks down the hallway with his forearm bloodied.

174. INT. ROOM, CRISTINA'S HOUSE – DAY

Paul and Cristina are lying naked on the bed. He is asleep. She, awake, ceaselessly looks at the half-open closet, where we can see Michael's clothing: shirts, a blue jacket, a pair of shoes, a suede jacket.

She looks distressed, but still kisses Paul tenderly on the cheek.

175. INT. KITCHEN, CRISTINA'S HOUSE – AFTERNOON

Paul is washing his hands in the sink.

> PAUL
> Do you want something to eat? I can whip up some pasta or a salad.

Cristina doesn't answer. Paul dries his hands and walks out of the kitchen.

176. INT. LIVING ROOM, CRISTINA'S HOUSE — CONTINUOUS

He enters the living room and sees Cristina cutting a line of cocaine on the coffee table.

> PAUL
> Cristina, please, don't . . .

Cristina ignores him and snorts the cocaine. She starts making another line, when Paul walks up to her and softly grabs her by the shoulder.

> Cristina, no . . .

Cristina shrugs her shoulder away from Paul's hand. She bends over to snort again and Paul stops her.

> You don't need this . . .

> CRISTINA
> How the fuck do you know what I need?

She snorts the cocaine, closes her eyes, waits a moment, gets up and leaves.

177. INT. RURAL CLINIC — DAY

Cristina is sitting in the waiting room. The nurse that drew blood in Scene 160 arrives to see her.

> NURSE
> Excuse me, ma'am, do you have a minute?

Cristina, very tired, slowly assents. The nurse sits next to her.

> CRISTINA
> How is Paul?

> NURSE
> No, not yet . . . (*A beat.*) Ms. Williams, we weren't able to use your blood for the transfusion.

CRISTINA

Why?

NURSE

We found high levels of illegal substances in your blood . . .
I think you're taking very high risks.

Cristina looks at her challengingly.

CRISTINA

That's my problem, isn't it?

NURSE

In your state I suggest you stop using these substances.

CRISTINA

What are you talking about?

NURSE

You're pregnant, didn't you know?

CRISTINA
(*disturbed*)

Are you sure?

NURSE

Confirmed by the lab.

Cristina puts her hand on her brow. The nurse gets up and looks at her compassionately.

You have to take care of yourself, ma'am. We'll tell you as
soon as Mr Rivers leaves the OR . . .

The nurse walks out. Cristina stays, alone, disconsolate, staring at the floor.

178. INT. KITCHEN, CRISTINA'S HOUSE — EVENING

Dusk. Cristina is sitting at the kitchen table, leaning on her elbows, hiding her face in her hands.

Paul walks in and sits down next to her. He watches her without saying a word. He stretches out his hand and caresses her temple.

Cristina moves away from his caress, stares at a fixed point and starts to talk, almost whispering.

CRISTINA

Katie could have lived . . .

Paul does not seem to understand what she is talking about.

PAUL

What did you say?

CRISTINA

Katie would be alive right now, but he left her there, lying in the street. He left the three of them like animals . . .

She starts to cry softly. Paul tries to console her by stroking her hair, but she moves away again.

Katie would be right here, with me . . . at least she would be here with me . . . and that bastard left and let her die in the street . . . and I haven't been able to go into their room . . . I just can't . . .

She collapses onto the table. Paul doesn't know what to do.

I'm in a prison and that son of a bitch is walking the streets . . .

PAUL

Since when is he free?

Cristina doesn't answer. She puts her hand on her brow and, without raising her head, starts speaking in a low voice.

CRISTINA

I'm going to kill him.

PAUL
(*astonished*)

What?

Cristina raises her hand and stares at him fixedly.

CRISTINA

I'm going to kill Jack Jordan . . . (*raising her voice*) I'm going to kill that son of a bitch . . .

127

Paul grabs her shoulders to calm her down.

Don't say that. Slow down, just slow down while you –

She shakes him off and gets up violently.

> CRISTINA

While I what? Huh? While I what?

Paul doesn't know what to say. Cristina looks at him furiously.

> PAUL

Take it easy . . .

> CRISTINA

Take it easy? My husband and my girls dead and I'm supposed to take it easy? (*A beat.*) This pain drops you on your knees and never lets you get up . . . never. Where do I crawl to hide from this pain? Tell me where?

Paul tries to hug her to calm her down, but she moves away and points at his heart with her index finger.

We have to kill him. You owe it to Michael. You've got his heart, you're in his house fucking his wife, sitting in the same chair he sat in . . . you have to kill him too, you owe it to him . . .

> PAUL

No, Cristina, not like this . . .

> CRISTINA

Then how? How?

She rubs her head with both her hands and then looks at him.

Katie died with red shoelaces on.

> PAUL
> (*disconcerted*)

What?

> CRISTINA

She hated red shoelaces and she asked me to buy her some blue ones and I never bought her the blue ones and she was wearing the red ones when she was run over . . . and she died looking at her fucking red shoelaces.

She collapses and starts crying desperately.

> We have to kill him, please, we have to. I can't be on my
> knees before this pain any more . . .

Paul holds her.

PAUL
(quietly)

> All right . . . All right . . .

179. EXT. DESERT — DAY

*From a wide shot we see Paul and Jack in the desert clearing from
Scene 132. Jack is kneeling and Paul is aiming at his head.*

PAUL

> You shouldn't have done it! Goddammit! Y-o-u
> s-h-o-u-l-d-n-'t . . .

Jack looks up; Paul still points.

JACK

> Done what?

PAUL

> Don't look at me.

He looks tense, about to shoot. Jack lowers his head.

JACK

> What do you want?

*Paul doesn't answer. Jack raises his head and looks him in the eyes.
Paul gets even more nervous.*

PAUL

> Close your eyes . . . Close them, goddammit!

*Jack does not comply. Paul squats, grabs some dirt and throws it in his
eyes. Jack opens and closes them with difficulty.*

> I said close them.

*Paul stretches the gun towards Jack, who lowers his head slightly,
resigning himself to death.*

Paul shoots the three shots to one side. Jack remains shaking, scared, breathing quickly.

> Murderer, you left two girls lying in the street . . . You let them die like dogs . . . I should have killed you . . .

Paul looks nervous, high-strung, terribly frightened.

> Leave now; don't even pick up your things from the motel.

JACK
What if I don't? Are you going to kill me?

PAUL
No, someone else will. If he won't, there'll be others. Leave, now.

He lowers the gun, turns around and walks away, leaving Jack kneeling in the desert. He starts to cry.

180. EXT. DESERT (CONTINUATION OF SCENE 90) — LATER

Paul walks, gun in hand. He doesn't look well. He stops and brings his hand to his heart. He winces in pain. He tries to walk a few more steps and stops again.

He has trouble breathing. He tries to go on and can't. He suddenly starts to vomit, retching violently.

181. INT. HOSPITAL ROOM — DAY

Mary is sitting alone and glum on a bed in the room, dressed in a white surgical gown.

Two nurses walk in pushing a gurney.

NURSE 1
Ready?

Mary nods. Nurse 2 points at the gurney.

NURSE 2
Lie down, please.

Mary gets up and walks over to the gurney.

> MARY
>
> How long do you think the operation will last?

> NURSE 2
>
> About three hours . . . (*A beat.*) Who'll be going with you?

Mary sighs and takes a while to answer.

> MARY
>
> Nobody; I came alone.

The nurse looks at her. With a gesture from her hand she tells Mary to get onto the gurney. Mary gets on and lies down. The nurses open the doors and wheel her out.

182. INT. WAITING ROOM, RURAL CLINIC — EVENING

Dusk. A few farmers are in the waiting room. Cristina is standing, looking at the desert through a window.

Jack, with his forearm bandaged, enters the waiting room and, hesitant, walks over to Cristina, who will not stop looking out of the window. He stands next to her without speaking. They are silent for a while.

> JACK
>
> I'm sorry . . .

She turns to look at him without speaking.

> Please forgive me . . .

She looks at him for a few more seconds and then looks back out at the desert. Jack takes half a step forward.

> There hasn't been one night, not one, I've been able to sleep through – not one minute I don't think about them.

His voice breaks up. Cristina turns to look at him, full of resentment and rage.

> CRISTINA
>
> You let them die lying in the street.

                           JACK
    I was scared, very scared.

Jack is desperate, on the verge of crying.

    Forgive me, please. If I could I would exchange my life for
    theirs . . .

Cristina starts crying quietly.

                          CRISTINA
    Your life is useless to me. It's just useless. (*A beat.*) Take
    your life somewhere else, if it's of any use to you.

                           JACK
    Please forgive me . . .

Cristina turns to look at him.

                          CRISTINA
    You forgive yourself . . . I've got nothing to do with you,
    I don't ever want to see you again.

*Jack wants to say something else, but she turns around and leaves him
alone before the farmers' furtive glances.*

183. INT. HIGHWAY MOTEL BATHROOM (CONTINUATION OF
SCENE 6) — DAY

*Cristina, dressed in black shorts and a T-shirt, is in the bathroom. She
opens a backpack and takes out a small baggie filled with cocaine. She
scoops some out with a bottlecap and snorts it. She sits on the toilet
cover, swallows and brings her hands to her head.*

She sighs, stands up and leaves the bathroom.

184. EXT. MOTEL — CONTINUOUS

*Cristina walks down the hallways looking for Paul. She spots him far
away, sitting on the old plastic chairs in front of the motel's empty
pool. Far away we hear the coos of a mourning dove.*

*She walks over to Paul and stands before him. He lifts his hand to
shield his brow from the sun vibrating behind her.*

CRISTINA

Where were you?

Paul doesn't answer. He pulls out a revolver from his waist, opens the cylinder and empties out three shells. He puts them on the glass top of a white iron table. Mesmerised, Cristina examines one of them.

Did you kill him?

Paul nods. Cristina grows pale and runs her left hand through her hair. They are silent.

Why didn't you wake me up?

Paul doesn't answer. He just looks out into the horizon.

What about the body?

PAUL

No one will ever find it . . .

CRISTINA

I want to see him dead . . . I want to see his fucking dead face . . .

Cristina's jaw shakes. Paul gets up and walks away without saying anything. Cristina is left alone next to the empty pool, on the brink of crying.

185. INT. MOTEL ROOM — MOMENTS LATER

Paul walks into the room and sits on the bed. He looks pale and has trouble breathing.

He grabs a pack of cigarettes and takes one out. He lights it and starts smoking anxiously. He starts to cough. He closes his eyes and takes a drag from the cigarette again.

Cristina walks in and sits down next to him and hugs him.

CRISTINA

I'm sorry . . . I'm sorry . . . I love you . . .

She kisses him on the mouth.

Let's go home . . . Let's get out of here.

Paul shakes his head.

PAUL

No. I don't feel well . . .

He coughs and lies on the bed. She caresses him, worried.

186. INT. MOTEL ROOM — NIGHT/DAWN

*Paul sleeps. Cristina, awake, stares at the ceiling. She looks restless.
Someone knocks. Cristina is startled. She wakes Paul by touching his
shoulder.*

CRISTINA
(*whispering*)

There's somebody outside.

*Paul wakes up. Another knock. He signals for her to be quiet.
Breathing with difficulty, he grabs the revolver and cautiously walks
towards the window. He looks out: nobody.*

*He opens the door and looks to one side: nobody. When he is about
to look the other way someone pushes him in. The shove makes him
stumble and he bumps into a table. A glass falls and breaks. Paul cuts
his feet.*

*Jack bursts into the room. (He is dressed as he was in Scene 172, where
he cut his forearm, which is still bleeding.)*

JACK
(*challenging*)

You wanted to kill me, motherfucker?

Cristina turns on the light.

(*screaming at Paul*) No one threatens me, bitch.

He pushes Paul again.

Shoot me, pussy . . . come on, shoot me . . .

He pushes him again and lifts up his arms challengingly.

Shoot me . . .

Cristina starts screaming at Paul.

CRISTINA

Why didn't you kill him? Why?

Paul turns to look at Cristina, but Jack pushes him.

JACK

Kill me, asshole . . .

CRISTINA

Kill him . . . kill him . . .

JACK

You don't have the balls, motherfucker.

CRISTINA

Shoot him . . .

Jack slaps the gun out of Paul's hands and headbutts him in the face, knocking him to the floor.

Jack turns to Cristina.

You killed my family, murderer . . .

JACK

Here I am . . .

He lifts up his arms defiantly. Cristina grabs the bedside lamp and throws it at him. Jack opens his arms and receives the blow, unfazed.

Cristina grows furious and grabs the poker from the run-down fake chimney and starts beating him furiously.

Jack withstands the first blow, but the second blow to his head makes him stagger.

Paul tries to get up but cannot. He starts yelling at Cristina from where he is.

PAUL

No, Cristina, no, you're going to kill him . . .

CRISTINA

Son of a bitch, son of a bitch . . .

PAUL

Stop, stop . . .

Paul, increasingly pale and weak, starts to breathe with great difficulty as he watches how Cristina furiously beats Jack, who falls on his knees.

No, Cristina, no . . .

Cristina seems ready to strike a mortal blow to his head. Paul gasps for air; he asphyxiates. His face shows great pain. He looks as if he is about to faint, to die.

He tries to yell at Cristina, but no longer has the strength. Lying on the floor he sees how she grips the poker to kill Jack. He grabs the gun, brings it to his chest with difficulty and shoots.

He falls back from the impact, which enters above his heart and blasts out his shoulder.

Cristina stops her attack and stares, stupefied, at Paul lying on the floor. Sudden silence. She drops the poker and runs to him. She bends down and tries to rouse him.

Jack sits up and stares at the scene, awestruck. Cristina turns to him as in Scene 20.

                    CRISTINA
                    (to Jack)
Call an ambulance.

Jack remains motionless, stunned.

(screaming) Call an ambulance, goddammit.

Jack is motionless for a few more seconds. Seeing that Jack does nothing, Cristina grabs Paul by the underarms and starts to drag him towards the door.

Jack seems to snap out of his stupefaction and runs to help her.

187. INT. CAR (CONTINUATION OF SCENE 50) — NIGHT/DAWN

Paul's head lies on Cristina's lap with open eyes. The car drives at full speed. His chest is totally bloodstained. All noise is far away, the voices are distant. Everything loses focus.

Fade out.

188. INT. INTENSIVE CARE UNIT PUBLIC SERVICE CLINIC — DAY

Again, Paul is in the intensive care unit from Scene 5, surrounded by the same dying patients.

> PAUL
> (*voice-over*)
> How many lives do we live? How many times do we get to die?

He looks around. He looks at the cancerous woman and the bandaged man staring at him, frightened.

> We all lose 21 grams when we die.

189. INT. SODA FOUNTAIN (THE SAME FROM SCENE 2) — NIGHT

Michael is standing in front of the register, paying. Katie is next to him, holding his hand, while Laura walks towards the door.

> MICHAEL
> Laura, stay inside, sweetie . . .

The girl smiles at her father and walks back to him.

> PAUL
> (*voice-over*)
> How much fits into 21 grams . . .?

190. EXT. BAR (SAME FROM SCENE 89) — NIGHT

Jack says goodbye to Brown in front of the same bar. He unlocks the silver Ford Lobo with the remote control, opens the door and gets in.

191. INT. SILVER FORD LOBO — CONTINUOUS

Jack closes the door, starts the engine and drives off.

> PAUL
> (*voice-over*)
> How much is lost . . .?

Cristina wraps herself in a towel and grabs her gym bag.

> CRISTINA
> (*to Claudia*)
>
> I'll call you.

When she is about to leave, Claudia, at the pool's edge, calls out to her.

> PAUL
> (*voice-over*)
>
> When do we lose 21 grams? . . .

> CLAUDIA
>
> Cristina . . .

Cristina turns around.

> Nothing, forget it . . .

Cristina smiles. Her sister blows her a kiss and goes on her way.

> PAUL
> (*voice-over*)
>
> How much goes with those 21 grams?

193. EXT. JACK'S HOUSE — NIGHT

Jack, bearded, dirty, dressed in a T-shirt and jeans arrives at the door to his house. He puts his hands under the rug, pulls out a key and opens the door. He walks in.

194. INT. ROOM JACK'S HOUSE — CONTINUOUS

Jack walks in and stands under the doorframe. Marianne is reading. She raises her eyes and sees him looking at her. They both look at each other.

> PAUL
> (*voice-over*)
>
> How much is gained?

195. INT. INSEMINATION ROOM — DAY

Mary is on a bed with her legs in the stirrups. The gynaecologist takes an inseminator, removes some semen from the jar from Scene 45 and is about to put it into Mary's vagina.

196. INT. HALLWAY CRISTINA'S HOUSE — AFTERNOON

Cristina is standing in front of the closed door to her daughters' room. She is slightly pregnant. She opens the door and walks in.

197. INT. CRISTINA'S HOUSE DAUGHTERS' ROOM — AFTERNOON

The girls' room is arranged the way it was the day they died. Several dolls are leaning on the pillows.

Cristina goes to sit on the edge of one of the beds, in a place similar to the one Jack sat on in his kids' room the day he killed the girls.

Cristina grabs one of the dolls and stares at it for a long time.

> PAUL
> (*voice-over*)
How much is gained?

198. INT. INTENSIVE CARE UNIT PUBLIC SERVICE CLINIC — DAY

Paul looks at a clock on the wall: 12:36. He then looks at the unconscious young woman.

> PAUL
> (*voice-over*)
21 grams . . . the weight of a stack of five nickels, the weight of a hummingbird, a chocolate bar . . . (*A beat.*) How much do 21 grams weigh?

He smiles slightly and closes his eyes. An alarm goes off. Nurses hurry towards him.

199. EXT. DESERT HIGHWAY — DAY

The sound of the alarm joins onto an empty highway in the desert. The sun beats down. Jack walks down the highway (dressed as he was in Scene 181 when he apologises to Cristina, and with his arm bandaged).

No cars pass. In the distance, he sees some vultures eating some roadkill on the pavement.

He draws near and sees that they are devouring a dead jackrabbit. He scares the vultures away and squats to look at it.

He puts his hand on its chest, strokes it and gazes at it for a long while.

Jack grabs the jackrabbit by one of its legs and pulls it to the edge of the road. He leaves the jackrabbit on the side of the highway without ceasing to look at it.

He suddenly hears a noise from the chaparral. He turns around and sees a coyote. Their eyes meet for a few seconds until the coyote trots away.

Jack watches it get lost amid the brush.

Fade out.

The End.

Photo Section